TRUMPLANDIA
UNMASKING POST-TRUTH AMERICA

TRUMPLANDIA

UNMASKING POST-TRUTH AMERICA

P.L. THOMAS

GARN PRESS
NEW YORK, NY

Published by Garn Press, LLC
New York, NY
www.garnpress.com

Book and cover design by Benjamin J. Taylor/Garn Press

First Edition, February 2017

Library of Congress Control Number: 2017932373

Publisher's Cataloging-in-Publication Data

Names: Thomas, Paul L.
Title: Trumplandia : unmasking post-truth America / P.L. Thomas.
Description: First edition. | New York : Garn Press, 2017. | Includes bibliographical references.
Identifiers: LCCN 2017932373 | ISBN 978-1-942146-55-1 (pbk.) | ISBN 978-1-942146-54-4 (Kindle ebook)
Subjects: LCSH: Civil disobedience. | Civil rights. | Fascism. | Government, Resistance to. | Racism. | Mass media and propaganda. | BISAC: POLITICAL SCIENCE / Corruption & Misconduct. | POLITICAL SCIENCE / Propaganda. | POLITICAL SCIENCE / Political Ideologies / Democracy. | POLITICAL SCIENCE / Political Ideologies / Fascism & Totalitarianism. | POLITICAL SCIENCE / Political Process / Media & Internet. | SOCIAL SCIENCE / Discrimination & Race Relations.
Classification: LCC JC328.3 .T487 2017 (print) | LCC JC328.3 (ebook) | DDC 323.73--dc23.
LC record available at https://lccn.loc.gov/2017932373

Contents

What Trumplandia Confirms about Republican Party, Christian Right, and White America

I just want to ask a question:
Who really cares, to save a world in despair?
Who really cares?
"Save the Children," Marvin Gaye

I was born and have lived my entire life in the cesspool of hypocrisy that is the Bible Belt—where conservative Republicanism and Christian values are thin veneer for hatred, bigotry, sexism, gun-lust, and enduring racism.

That hypocrisy failed me and then as a young adult and throughout my life I have been taught critical love and kindness by great writers and thinkers: Kurt Vonnegut, Eugene V. Debs,

Alice Walker, Toni Morrison, Langston Hughes, and the greatest witness of all, James Baldwin.

With the election of Donald Trump as the U.S. president, the entire nation has before it this reality: Trumplandia confirms that the Republican Party, Christian Right, and white America have abdicated all rights to any moral authority.

First, despite efforts by mainstream media and pundits to argue otherwise, Trump and his rhetoric are continuations of central efforts by the Republican Party reaching back at least to Reagan: "tough on crime" as code for racist beliefs about blacks and Latinx, "build a wall" as just more xenophobia, and anti-government ranting as code for denying "free" offerings to the "lazy" people of color and "illegal immigrants."

Trump's Republicanism is directly in line with Reagan Republicanism. The only real difference is Trump's outlandish and brash admissions *aloud* of the very worst of the Republican Party, such as calling Mexicans rapists and murderers. Traditional Republicans only hint at such.

Even more important is that the overwhelming support for Trump by the Christian Right[1] is stunningly damning:

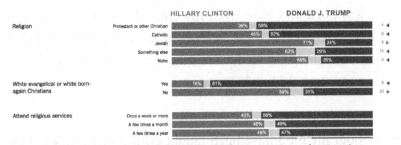

Election 2016: Exit Polls (*The New York Times* 8 November 2016)

For eight years, Barack Obama and his family—despite a history of being practicing Christians, despite Obama himself offering several eloquent and *Christian* speeches and hymns in times of tragedy, and despite Obama and his family living essentially good (read: Christian) lives—the Christian Right, and Trump, have refuted Obama's Christianity and used accusations of his being a Muslim as a slur.

Yet, Trump's hedonism, adultery, sexual assault, profane discourse, hate speech, sexism, and rapacious behavior as a business man and pseudo-billionaire[2], for the Christian Right, prove to be just fine.

Trumplandia has exposed there is nothing "Christian" or "right" about the Christian Right.

Finally, however, the most damning and least addressed consequence of Trumplandia is what it has exposed about white America, who overwhelmingly supported Trump:

> As expected, Trump did best among white voters without a college degree, beating Clinton by the enormous margin of 72 percent to 23 percent. Trump also won among white, non-college women 62 to 34 percent and white college-educated men, 54 to 39 percent. Among white voters, Clinton only won among women with a college degree by a 51 to 45 percent margin. Interestingly, among white voters, there is no evidence in the exit poll that income affected the likelihood that they supported Trump.[3]

The conventional wisdom being promoted by whitewashed mainstream media[4] is that the working and middle class have been abandoned by Democrats and the U.S. government; yet, exit polls show that the two lowest income categories chose Clinton by a slim majority (certainly skewed, however, by people of color over-represented in these groups, revealing how the media is mostly worried about "working class" and "middle class" only as that relates to whites):

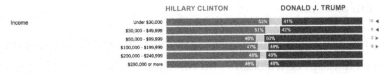

Election 2016: Exit Polls (*The New York Times* 8 November 2016)

Both sets of exit data from CBS and NYT, then, suggest that Trump's support has more to do with race than disgruntled working class whites being ignored and disenfranchised. Actually, mainstream media have their argument backward because Trumplandia confirms that white America has abandoned commitments to *equity for all*—not that any political party or the U.S. government has abandoned white America.

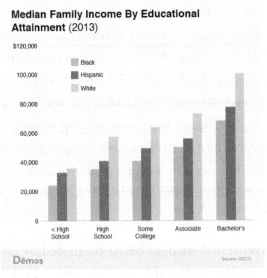

Bruenig, 24 October 2014[5]

As these two Bruenig graphics demonstrate, the problem is not the "hurting white working/middle class" but racially inequitable America.

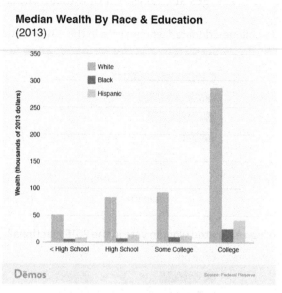

Bruenig, 24 October 2014

The America where race and gender create exponential inequity:

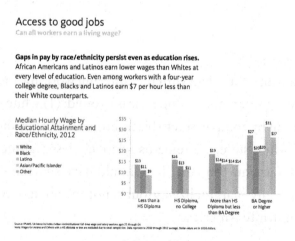

Policy Link[6]

As a powerful contrast to the white male and female support to Trump, note that black women were by far least likely to vote for Trump—and they have the greatest reason to be disenfranchised (the lowest wages at every level of education, above):

How did non-college-educated women vote in the 2016 elections?

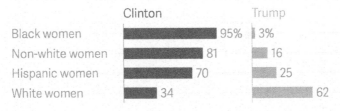

ATLAS | Data: National Election Pool

Quartz[7]

How did college educated women vote in the 2016 elections?

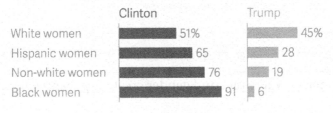

ATLAS | Data: National Election Pool

Quartz

The ultimate problem with the suffering working and middle class white argument for Trump's rise is twofold: (1) white suffering may exist, but by comparison to black/brown suffering and gender suffering, white suffering remains relatively less significant, and (2) if whites are hurting, that fact should have spurred solidarity with historically marginalized groups, not the antagonism being heard from white America.

If white America ever really believed in the melting pot,

believed in a country of immigrants, believed in equity for all, that may have existed in some distant and idealized past when white America saw that pot melting disparate whites into one homogenous white: equity for *all who look like us* (white).

Trumplandia is a white response (whitelash[8]), not *from* working and middle class suffering, but *against* rising demands by oppressed groups (#BlackLivesMatter, Colin Kaepernick, gender neutral restrooms, marriage equity, immigration reform, etc.) for equity for all.

The only thing whites are poised to lose is their unearned privilege, but the rise of white support of Trump confirms that whites see their privilege as more important to preserve than equity for all is to attain.

"Make America Great Again" is slogan-as-code for maintaining white (and male) privilege.

In the tumultuous world faced by Marvin Gaye—especially war torn—he sang:

But who really cares?
Who's willing to try?
To save our world
To save our sweet world
To save a world
That is destined…to die. ("Save the Children")

Trumplandia is a defiant "Not us" from white America—and efforts to whitewash that callousness as economic angst is further proof that the dirtiest word in the U.S. to utter is "racism" because of the delicate sensibilities of the most powerful people in the country.

The Roots of Trumplandia: "What You Say about Somebody Else, Anybody Else, Reveals You"

In *Take this Hammer* (1963), James Baldwin speaks pointedly and thoughtfully about "Who is the Nigger?" In his explication of the racial slur rendered taboo, Baldwin explains that "What you say about somebody else, anybody else, reveals you." Baldwin asks his listeners to turn the racism and demonizing of people positioned as "Others" back on those using language as both a sword and a mask.

Often, racial slurs as taboo words have resulted in an ironic silencing of discussions of race as well. Polite company—that middle-class norm of civility—will not allow racial slurs, but that censoring of a word also becomes a more insidious form of oppression, a verbal shielding of the remaining racism that strangles the American pursuit of democracy.

Nearly fifty years after *Hammer*, during the 2012 Republican primaries for president, Americans found themselves confronted by the most corrosive forms of racism in the candidacy of Newt Gingrich, but few strayed outside the confines of civility to name it for what it was.

As Republicans chose to support Donald Trump, the discussion below of Gingrich in 2012 remains relevant since Trump has followed an even more aggressively racist and fascist pattern rooted in Gingrich's campaign strategies.

"I'm Going to Continue to Help Poor People Learn How to Get a Job"

During Gingrich's rise to winning the South Carolina presidential primary in January 2012, Gingrich built a steady platform about "poor people"—including the following:

- Repeating the refrain that Obama is the "food stamp president."

- Calling for "poor children" to be given work in schools as janitors because:

  > "Really poor children in really poor neighborhoods have no habits for working and have nobody around them who works. So they literally have no habit of showing up on Monday," Gingrich told more than 500 employees inside the Nationwide Insurance lunchroom, NBC News reported. "So they literally have no habit of showing up on Monday. They have no habit of staying all day. They have no habit of 'I do this and you

give me cash,' unless it's illegal."[9]

- Assuming the pose of professor and job creator by announcing he was "…going to continue to help poor people learn how to get a job, learn how to get a better job, and someday learn how to own the job."[10]

Gingrich's racism and his speaking to the racism of his constituency were in many ways more insidious than the racial slur confronted by Baldwin in 1963 because Gingrich's ploy allowed him to mask his intent one or two layers beneath his words. "Food stamps," "janitor," "no habit" (laziness), and "illegal" trigger the racial stereotypes that drive racism—stereotypes that have no basis in fact, but remain robust in America's social norms and uncritical acceptance of myths such as the culture of poverty.

As a fifty-plus-year-old white man living my entire life in the South, I am well acquainted with the pervasive direct racism as well as the wink-wink-nod-nod racism not just a legacy of the South but a daily reality remaining today. As Gingrich mined and as Obama remained mostly silent on that racism, Americans and their leaders must confront the realities of the land of the free and the home of the brave:

- Males constitute about half the U.S. population, but represent by 10 to 1 the prison population; white men outnumber black men about 6 to 1, but black men fill U.S. prisons at a rate 6 to 1 compared to white men.

- According to 2005 research by Walter Gilliam[11], prekindergarten expulsion rates mirror U.S. prison dynamics: "Black boys receive less attention, harsher punishments, and lower grades in school than their White counterparts":

African-American preschoolers were about twice as likely to be expelled as European-American (both Latino and non-Latino) preschoolers and over five times as likely as Asian-American preschoolers. Boys were expelled at a rate over 4½ times that of girls. The increased likelihood of boys to be expelled over girls was similar across all ethnicities, except for African-Americans ($?2 = 25.93$, $p < .01$), where boys accounted for 91.4% of the expulsions.

- Childhood poverty has accelerated in the U.S. (well over 20%) and ranks far below countries similar to the U.S. throughout the world—see UNICEF Innocenti Report Cards for 2002[12], 2005[13] and 2007[14].

- The wealth gap has increased significantly among racial groups:

  The racial wealth gap has been enormous ever since the Census Bureau began measuring it 25 years ago. But it has never been larger than today. The median wealth of a white family is now at least 20 times higher than that of a black family and 18 times that of a Latino family, according to an analysis by the Pew Research Center.[15]

- The welfare myth remains powerful but also inaccurate—specifically in terms of who receives food stamps:

  Gingrich, meanwhile has been criticized not only for singling out Obama as the "food stamp president" but for specifically linking the program to minorities. The NAACP and the National Urban League sharply criticized him for comments in early January that "the African-American community should demand paychecks and not be satisfied with food stamps," accusing him of feeding stereotypes about the black poor. In fact, 22% of SNAP recipients are black, compared to 36% for whites, 10% for Latinos and 18% from unknown racial backgrounds.[16]

- Equity, especially among the races, and upward mobility have eroded in the U.S., often dwarfed by greater equity and upward mobility in other countries. Timothy Smeeding explains in "Canada's Economic Mobility Creates a Land of Opportunity" (*The New York Times*):

  Higher levels of economic inequality are associated with lower rates of mobility. But children are more upwardly mobile in some nations than in others. How do countries like Canada, with above-average inequality and above-average child poverty rates, do so well on mobility outcomes compared with the United States? Canada has more effective public investments in education, including nearly universal preschool, effective secondary schools and high rates of college completion. And the Canadians are much more generous to low- and middle-income families, including child allowances and tuition breaks for university education.

- While "No Excuses" education reformers simultaneously

decry public education a historical failure and the sole mechanism for social reform, children of color and children in poverty are routinely assigned to classrooms taught by the least experienced and un-/under-qualified teachers— including a rise in hiring Teach for America (TFA) recruits to staff high-poverty schools and in corporate charter schools that are re-segregating public education.

The reality of racism and inequity in America is being ignored, and politicians, such as Gingrich, bait racists and perpetuate racism, directly and indirectly. Room for Debate (*The New York Times*) includes George Lakoff identifying why and how politicians continue to misrepresent the state of America:

> But more often politicians lie to protect or advance what they see as a moral endeavor (e.g., the invasion of Iraq, Reagan's war on nonexistent 'welfare queens, Johnson on the Tonkin Gulf). In the conservative moral system, the highest value is protecting and extending the moral system itself. When conservative icons or ideas themselves are threatened, it is not uncommon for conservative politicians to lie in their defense (Reagan never raised taxes; there's no evidence for global warming; "government takeover").

It is politically advantageous to claim that America is post-racial, that America has achieved equity, but as the evidence above shows, those claims are political lies.

We may say that Gingrich's campaign strategy included race-baiting or class warfare, but that would be yet more masking and avoiding the harsh reality that Gingrich's strategy was racism—and it often worked.

To paraphrase and extend Baldwin's perceptive understanding of a racial slur, what Gingrich said about poor people was telling us about *him*, and by association, *those who voted for him.*

Racism remains a vivid and crippling scar on the American character now moving into the Trumplandia era, and America needs leadership and voices that will name that reality and call for a commitment to *seeking* the ideals of equity and post-*racism* America. But that will never occur if we hide behind the masks of middle-class civility and political expediency that claim we have achieved the ideals we debase every day.

Welcome to South Carolina: Where "Bless Your Heart" Means "Go to Hell"

I zipped through John Saward's "Keeping It Casual: A Day with South Carolina's 21st Century Racists," and then posted the article on Facebook with "Painful but real about SC."

Little did I know that a former student was involved in Saward's interview and even captured in the article's main photograph. Luckily, she explained to me that Saward came off as looking to paint as negative a picture of South Carolinians as possible, prompting me to consider more carefully what I had posted and why.

I did add this *New York Times* analysis of who supports Trump in the South[17], confirming, I think, my larger point—even acknowledging that Saward had an agenda regardless of what he found. So my much more careful point is two-fold:

1. Outsiders coming to the South in order to make us look bad is wrong and upsetting for those such as me from The South.

2. But the ugly, ugly truth is they don't even have to try to make us look bad because bigotry, nastiness, and racism/sexism are still proudly embraced by way too many and *tolerated by way too many more*—and that ugliness is usually all justified by Bible thumping, making it all the worse.

This brings me to the two disjointed stereotypes about the South—one that praises us for Southern Hospitality and the other that demonizes us as cross-burning, toothless rednecks. These caricatures are partially grounded in truth, but the cartoonishness of both makes the mistake that Ta-Nehisi Coates addressed in "This Town Needs a Better Class of Racist" about "oafish racists":

> The problem with Cliven Bundy isn't that he is a racist but that he is an oafish racist. He invokes the crudest stereotypes, like cotton picking. This makes white people feel bad. The elegant racist knows how to injure non-white people while never summoning the specter of white guilt. Elegant racism requires plausible deniability, as when Reagan just happened to stumble into the Neshoba County fair and mention state's rights. Oafish racism leaves no escape hatch, as when Trent Lott praised Strom Thurmond's singularly segregationist candidacy.

> Elegant racism is invisible, supple, and enduring. It disguises itself in the national vocabulary, avoids epithets and didacticism.

The South broadly and South Carolina specifically are not uniquely a region and state that represent the corrosive impact of virulent hypocrisy, but both are significant breeding grounds for hatred, racism, classism, homophobia, and sexism shielded by a nasty veneer of Bible thumping.

So if you are just visiting, "Bless your heart" may mean "Bless your heart," but it may also mean "Go to hell" (or possibly more accurately, "You are going to hell [and I'm not]").

With SC Republicans supporting Trump as they did Newt Gingrich, as a native South Carolinian and an unabashed redneck, I am forced once again (and this is a daily, if not hourly, experience) to note that Trump is exposing that the so-called Religious Right is neither religious (in the moral/ethical sense), nor right.

Trump uses brazen lies and lies that are grounded in hatred to attract a legion of voters who once called themselves the Moral Majority; and in fact, those iterations—Moral Majority, Religious Right, Evangelicals—have always been as nasty as they are currently being by aligning themselves with Trump—a cartoon in a suit and a wig who is even more outlandish than the imagined future in *Idiocracy*.

Trump, in fact, is the perfect lightning rod for the very worst the South has to offer—the uneducated fundamentalists who cling to conviction even when it is self-defeating. The brutal irony of the South is that the tired Republican ploy of making Americans afraid of terrorists (non-Americans) and whites afraid of people of color is that one need not live long in the South to know first-hand the reality of what is immediately dangerous for anyone—your own damn family, and people like you or that you know.

As I examined during the most recent debate about finally removing the Confederate battle flag from state house grounds, if you really want to understand the South, investigate the nonsensical rallying cry of flag supporters, "Heritage, not hate."[18]

But I want to return to the point raised by Coates because

it is not the KKK defenders who are the problem in the South (and this appears to be the narrative Saward was going to write regardless of what he found), but the same ideologies resting in the breasts of working class, middle class, and affluent Southerners who, like Emily in William Faulkner's "A Rose for Emily," cannot and will not let go of our tarnished traditions in order to build a more perfect union.

The problem is that many in the South passionately wave the flag and thump the Bible without a clue to what either means, and without a moment of their lives spent honoring either.

Instead, the flag waving and Bible thumping are used as weapons to smear good people and to deny *others* life, liberty, and the pursuit of happiness.

Again, this is not unique to the South, but as a Southerner, it kills my soul that this is too often the South and none need come here to make any of that up.

See Also:

Eternal Fascism and the Southern Ideology, Jeremy Brunger

Are Racially Inequitable Outcomes Racist?

Among what may seem to be marginally related policies and conditions, these all have one startling thing in common—grade retention, school discipline, NCAA athletics, incarceration, "grit," "no excuses," zero-tolerance, high-stakes testing (such as the SAT and ACT), charter schools and school choice—and that commonality is observable racially inequitable outcomes that are significantly negative for blacks.

My own experiences with exploring and confronting race and racism through my public writing has shown that many people vigorously resist acknowledging racism and will contort themselves in unbelievable ways to avoid accepting facts and data that show racism exists.

Common responses include "I am not a racist," "I am sure the people who started X didn't *intend* to be racist," "White people experience racism too," and "Everyone has the same opportunities in this country."

And while I continue to compile a stunning list of ways in which racial inequity and racism profoundly impact negatively black people, resistance to terms such as "white privilege" and "racism" remain robust.

In the wake of the 2016 NCAA Final Four, Patrick Hruby's "Four Years A Student-Athlete: The Racial Injustice of Big-Time College Sports" has attempted a similar tactic I have used in order to unmask the racial inequity in college athletics by carefully working readers through the evidence in order to come to an uncomfortable conclusion about the financial exploitation of college athletes (money-making sports being disproportionately black) by the NCAA and colleges/universities (leadership and those profiting being overwhelmingly white) along racial lines:

> **Understand this: there's nothing inherently racist about amateurism itself.** And there's no reason to believe that its defenders and proponents—including current NCAA president Mark Emmert—are motivated by racial animus….

> And yet, while the NCAA's intent is color-blind, the impact of amateurism is anything but. In American law, there is a concept called *adverse impact*, in which, essentially, some facially neutral rules that have an unjustified adverse impact on a particular group can be challenged as discriminatory….Similarly, sociologists speak of *structural racism* when analyzing public policies that have a disproportionately negative impact on minority individuals, families, and communities. State lottery systems that essentially move money from predominantly lower-class African-American ticket buyers to predomi-

nantly middle-and-upper-class white school districts fit the bill; so does a War on Drugs that disproportionately incarcerates young black men; so does a recent decision by officials in Maricopa County, Arizona, to drastically cut the number of presidential primary polling stations in and around Phoenix, which unnecessarily made voting far more difficult for the residents of a non-white majority city.

Big-time college sports fall under the same conceptual umbrella. Amateurism rules restrain campus athletes—and only campus athletes, not campus musicians or campus writers—from earning a free-market income, accepting whatever money, goods, or services someone else wants to give them. And guess what? In the revenue sports of Division I football and men's basketball, where most of the fan interest and television dollars are, the athletes are disproportionately black.

And herein lies the problem with refusing to equate racially inequitable outcomes with racism. Hruby's detailed unmasking of the NCAA came also during the troubling rise of Trump in presidential politics—another marker for how many scramble to find any cause other than racism.

Trump's rise is not exclusively the result of overt and unexamined racism, but a significant amount of his success is easily traced to a wide spectrum of racism.

However, from the rise of Trump to the so-called popularity of charter schools to the school-to-prison pipeline and to the spread of third-grade retention policies, all of these and more are fueled by racism because racism, we must acknowledge, is most insidious when it isn't overt, when the racist person or the racist act is unconscious, unacknowledged.

The impact of racism in NCAA sports, as Hruby details, is the *elegant racism* Ta-Nahisi Coates unpacked when Donald Sterling became the NBA's face for *oafish racism* (along with Clive Bundy in popular culture).

What has occurred in the U.S. since the mid-1960s is an end to placard racism, the end of "White Only" signs on bathroom and restaurant doors.

What has not occurred in the U.S. yet is an end to seeing black boys as significantly older than their biological ages, an end to tracking black children into segregated schools and reductive courses, an end to incarcerating black men—and this is a list that could go on for several pages.

Racial (and class) equity will never occur in the U.S. until the white power structure admits that racially inequitable outcomes are in fact racist.

White privilege is a powerful narcotic that numbs white elites to the harm that privilege causes black and brown people, but it is also a powerful narcotic that pits poor whites against black and brown people because poor whites believe their whiteness gives them the chance at great wealth held by only a few.

That the NCAA maintains a structure within which black athletes produce wealth enjoyed almost exclusively by white elites is an undeniable fact and a startling example of the *elegant racism* eroding the soul of a free people—an elegant racism eating at the roots of public education, the judicial system, the economic system, and nearly every aspect of the country.

Racially inequitable outcomes *are racist*, and this must be admitted in order to be confronted and then to be eliminated.

Scalia's Racism Exposes Higher Education's Negligence

It is a nearly imperceptibly short stroll from Donald Trump to Supreme Court Justice Antonin Scalia. The arrogance of power is disturbing for its privilege and bigotry, but exponentially so for the cavalier brashness and absence of self-awareness.

Regardless of the position of power, Scalia's racist pronouncements[19] about the proper place of black students in higher education (again, a short stroll from Supreme Court Justice Clarence Thomas's rejecting affirmative action[20], which he himself used during his journey to the highest bench) are inexcusable.

However, there is another story Scalia is inadvertently exposing: the negligence of higher education to *teach* the students who walk the halls and sit in the classrooms after being admitted.

First, let me pull away from that specific claim to a broader pet peeve of mine: remediation.

Throughout formal education at every level from pre-K through undergraduate (and even graduate) education, students are commonly labeled as remedial (a designation that suggests the students are not at the proper level for the course they are taking) and thus need some additional services.

This is total hogwash. *All students are remedial, and no students are remedial.* You see, the essential role of a teacher and formal education is to identify what knowledge and skills students have as well as what knowledge and skills students lack (or need developing), and *then to teach those students in that context.*

So let's return to higher education in the U.S.—where attending college is not a basic right and is often a tremendous burden on students and their families.

A significant number of students are admitted to colleges and universities for the benefit of the institution (full-pay students and athletes, as the most prominent examples). Often, these populations fall into the deficit category of "remedial," or would be the exact type of student Scalia has now further marginalized with the damning blanket of racism.

From the most accessible (in terms of admissions) public colleges to the most selective private colleges, access to higher education in the U.S. is nonetheless selective. In other words, colleges accept students (and reject others) under the tacit contract that each belongs there and that the university will provide the education for which the student (or someone) is paying.

Again, I have taught public school in the impoverished rural South and a selective liberal arts university. Those two contrasting settings have shown me that I often taught diligently at the high school setting with little concrete evidence I was successful (many students still scored low in standardized testing), but that I could (if I chose to do so) do very little with my college students (extremely bright and motivated) and there would still be ample evidence of success.

And herein lies the issue no one is talking about beneath the embarrassment of Justice Scalia's comments: vulnerable populations of students admitted to colleges and universities (often black, brown, poor, and English language learners)—those who need higher education the most, in fact—are being neglected by the very institutions who admit them, often after actively recruiting them (again, the athletes).

I teach two sections of writing-intensive first-year seminars each academic year. The greatest difference between my successful and struggling students is *their experiences and relative privilege* before attending my university.

Successful students have "done school" in ways suitable for college expectations before while struggling students rarely have.

Too often, echoing Scalia, many in higher education shake their collective heads and mutter these students shouldn't be "at *our* college."

Too often, higher education is a place that simply has no interest in teaching—opting instead for gate-keeping (masking privilege with the bigoted allure of measurable qualifications), housing students for a few years, and then taking credit for the outcomes.

Scalia's bigotry, like Trump's, is repulsive, but let's not fool ourselves that it is somehow unique to a few privileged apples (who Ta-Nehisi Coates calls "oafish racist[s]").

That bigotry is institutionalized all across the U.S., and our places of higher education too often are those institutions.

Baldwin's "Notes for a Hypothetical Novel": "We made the world we're living in and we have to make it over"

At first, I think, most relatively reasonable people believed the 2016 Republican field for president was amusing, a harmless opening act to the *very serious politics* that would befall us when the time came.

But with Donald Trump winning primary after primary, and with many *very serious pundits* conceding that Trump could be the Republican nominee, this harmless opening act turned decidedly ugly.

A testament to his genius as well as a damning statement about the recalcitrant nature of the U.S., James Baldwin's work offers disturbing commentaries on our present, especially in the context of Trump's blatant fascism and bigotry along with the so-called mainstream Republican candidates' coded fascism and bigotry.

Baldwin's "Notes for a Hypothetical Novel" proves to be one such insightful work.

In this address, Baldwin admits early, "I'm certain that there is something which unites all the Americans in this room, though I can't say what it is." Then, he launches into speculating aloud about a hypothetical novel.

"[B]ecause I am an American writer," he explains, "my subject and my material inevitably has to be a handful of incoherent people in an incoherent country," setting up his explicating more carefully later "incoherent."

This novel, he poses, would be grounded in his life, the people and places he knows, starting with his birth into the Negro (Harlem) Renaissance:

> This Negro Renaissance is an elegant term which means that white people had then discovered that Negroes could act and write as well as sing and dance and this Renaissance was not destined to last very long. Very shortly there was to be a depression and the artistic Negro, or the noble savage, was to give way to the militant or the new Negro; and I want to point out something in passing which I think is worth our time to look at, which is this: that the country's image of the Negro, which hasn't very much to do with the Negro, has never failed to reflect with a kind of frightening accuracy the state of mind of the country.

Baldwin refutes writing a typical coming-of-age novel before delving deeper into race and Harlem itself: "Because, remember

that we're projecting a novel, and Harlem is in the course of changing all the time, very soon there won't be any white people there,
and this is also going to have some effect on the people in my story."

Next, Baldwin comes to terms with the white world. "Now
this white world which I was just encountering was," he explains,
"just the same, one of the forces that had been controlling me
from the time I opened my eyes on the world"—building to his
larger realization:

> Anyway, in the beginning I thought that the white world
> was very different from the world I was moving out of
> and I turned out to be entirely wrong. It seemed different.
> It seemed safer, at least the white people seemed safer.
> It seemed cleaner, it seemed more polite, and, of course,
> it seemed much richer from the material point of view.
> But I didn't meet anyone in that world who didn't suffer
> from the very same affliction that all the people I had
> fled from suffered from and that was that they didn't
> know who they were. They wanted to be something that
> they were not. And very shortly I didn't know who I was,
> either. I could not be certain whether I was really rich
> or really poor, really black or really white, really male or
> really female, really talented or a fraud, really strong or
> merely stubborn. In short, I had become an American.

As relevant today as then, Baldwin answers "What does it
mean to be an American?" with race, noting "[t]he fact of color
has a relevance objectively and some relevance in some other way,
some emotional relevance and not only for the South."

To be American, it seems, Baldwin confronts the power of race
and the paradox of being an American (which he argues joins black

and white)—all of which comes to his concern with our genuine selves, the risk of being our genuine selves: "I mean that in order to have a conversation with someone you have to reveal yourself."

Along with "the fact of race," Baldwin argues "to try and find out what Americans mean is almost impossible because there are so many things they do not want to face."

To be American is to live with delusion:

[I]t seems to me that the myth, the illusion, that this is a free country, for example, is disastrous....

There is an illusion about America, a myth about America to which we are clinging which has nothing to do with the lives we lead and I don't believe that anybody in this country who has really thought about it or really almost anybody who has been brought up against it— and almost all of us have one way or another— this collision between one's image of oneself and what one actually is is always very painful and there are two things you can do about it, you can meet the collision head-on and try and become what you really are or you can retreat and try to remain what you thought you were, which is a fantasy, in which you will certainly perish.

And as we faced in the U.S. during the 2016 presidential campaign the rise of a candidate more outlandish and nastier than a cult-classic film such as *Idiocracy*, Baldwin's concluding comment could not be more apt: "A country is only as good— I don't care now about the Constitution and the laws, at the moment let us leave these things aside— a country is only as strong as the people who make it up and the country turns into what the people want it to become."

And as Americans chose Trump, we must realize: "We made the world we're living in and we have to make it over."

See Also:

The Weight of James Arthur Baldwin, Rachel Kaadzi Ghansah

The Irrational Expectation of Rational Behavior

What do debates about "no zero" policies in schools and the presidential run of Donald Trump have in common?

They expose the irrational expectation of rational behavior.

Several years ago, I was having a casual conversation with an economics professor, and during that exchange, it hit me that his entire premise was based on a belief that consumers are rational—a faith that the market hinges on a careful analysis of *Consumer Report* before each purchase.

I have since seen some critiques of economics because of the use of rationality in the models, but I also witness this daily: people adamant that zeroes teach children lessons, forcing them to comply; people who call for the death penalty and tougher laws as deterrents; and now seemingly reasonable people espousing a series of reasons for supporting Trump.

And that brings me to the somewhat baffling fact that John Oliver has once again posed through comedy an incredibly rational deconstruction of those pro-Trump claims. But here is the problem—from demanding we continue to give students zeroes to calls for tougher laws and the death penalty to dispassionately dismantling the lunacy that is Trump—*rational has no impact on the irrational, and most people are irrational.*

Purchases are often impulse buys, children and teens do not see school or the future in rational ways, crimes are often crimes of passion or desperation, and people supporting Trump are the very embodiments of irrational.

This realization is an ironic gift of having been born and raised in the South where there is no rational connection between what the self-defeating South believes and the reality of the world around us: the Bible-belt is anything but Christian, and our region is crippled by racism and poverty, but we wallow in hating "government."

None of this makes any rational sense.

Now sitting before us is the Trump phenomenon to make all this desperately clear—Trump is the ultimate Teflon candidate who makes Reagan seem in hindsight less of a cartoon than he was.

If direct associations between the KKK and Trump had no impact on his appeal as a candidate, there was no hope that Oliver's very careful and detailed dismantling of the facade of Trump would resonate—even if the anemic mainstream media did their job.

Despite what religious texts or science fiction seems to show, the apocalypse is a slow unveiling, something only recognized well past its fruition. The U.S. has always been an irrational belief culture, and we have witnessed Trump cashing in on that in a way that makes reality TV, reality.

I Didn't Mean to Be Politically Prescient, But ...

This is a poem I wrote in 2012, mostly out of a growing cynicism about mainstream politics. However, it appears that the 2016 presidential season proved me to be far more prescient than I intended:

choice (Vote!)

Circus was a festive land, especially at Festival.
Every citizen was proud to be part of the 3Rings.

This day the Tent was snaked with lines to vote,
and he had learned the slogans by heart as a child:

"Your Ring, Your Clown, Your Choice" and
"A Choice Is a Terrible Thing to Waste."

So he waited his turn to choose between two cards—
Ring 1: Barnum Party Blue, Ring 2: Bailey Party Red.

Either choice he already knew, but dared not utter:
When he chose his card and returned to the elephants,

he remained forever Carny1691 with a shovel because
nothing was ever different behind the paint of a Clown.

O Captain America! Our Captain America!

Every woman adores a Fascist,
The boot in the face, the brute
Brute heart of a brute like you.
"Daddy," Sylvia Plath

Camille Paglia in "Zombie time at campaign Hillary" has confronted her own prescience about the direct line from Arnold Schwarzenegger being elected governor of California to Donald Trump now being a successful candidate for president: "This is how fascism is born."

And while these political realities—possibly catastrophic to a people clinging to life, liberty, and the pursuit of happiness—will likely *not* receive very much attention by the mainstream public, please don't fuck with an iconic comic book superhero:

The goal, of course, is to shock readers into buying the

next issue, and presumably that's what comics scribe Nick Spencer and his colleagues at Marvel Comics hoped to do when they executed a final-page revelation in last Wednesday's *Captain America: Steve Rogers No. 1*: We learned that Cap is actually ... *evil?* The Star-Spangled Avenger uttered the words, "Hail Hydra," the fascistic slogan of longtime villain collective Hydra. Say it ain't so![21]

Comic books (and more recently graphic novels and the film adaptation of superhero comic books) have always been both a reflection of and fuel for pop culture in the U.S.

And the primary subgenre of comic books, superhero narratives, has done far more to perpetuate the very worst of our society than to confront or seek to rise above xenophobia, racism, sexism, homophobia, and warmongering.

Marvel Comics claimed the comic book throne in the 1960s—over long-time powerhouse DC—but has since experienced a renaissance through film adaptations. Iron Man and Captain America, for example, have recaptured the public's imagination—but only a few have offered that their appeal is strongly grounded in our militarism, our patriotism that is strongly tainted with nationalism and even jingoism.

These film adaptations have carried on a tradition of the comic book industry—one that is primarily market driven: the reboot.

Now, however, pop culture has two competing set of fans, clashing nerdoms—those who worship at the altar of the comic book universe(s) and those who worship at the altar of the film universe(s).

Captain America being outed as a life-long fascist, then, in the pages of the comic book reboot of Steve Rogers as Captain America alongside Sam Wilson as the replacement Captain America (see below) has drawn the ire of fans.

However, that anger lacks a grasp of both the history of Captain America and that Captain America has always been *our* fascist.

The general public in the U.S. suffers under a lazy understanding of terminology—such as "communism," "socialism," and "fascism"—and under the weight of an idealized (and misleading) faith in capitalism, one that confuses the "free market" with freedom, liberty.

The horrors of fascism include its embracing totalitarianism and militarism in order to sustain corporatism. It is fascism, in fact, that is perfectly reflected in Captain America.

In a chapter I recently completed[22], I examine race in superhero comic books, and focus on the ascension of Sam Wilson, black and formerly The Falcon, to being Captain America. In that discussion, I researched and unpacked the history of Captain America. Below is an excerpt of that unpacking.

Comic Book Superheroes: From Gods to White Knights

While gaining a much larger cultural status because of the rise of Marvel films, Captain America may best represent how superhero comics represent race and racism—as the ultimate White Knight. "Captain America, an obviously Aryan ideal," McWilliams[23] poses, "has always had a curious relationship with racial ideals" (p. 66). In fact, Golden Age (from the 1940s), Silver Age (later mid-twentieth century), and contemporary Captain America each represents well the comic book industry (and Marvel Comics specifically) as well as how popular culture reflects/perpetuates and confronts race and racial stereotypes.

As superhero archetype, Captain America embodies the masked duality[24], the white ideal, the masculine norm, and the periodic rebooting of superhero origins as part marketing strategy and part recalibration that helps mend the tear between the official *canon* of the comic book universe with the changing real world. The rebooted origin stories of Captain America/Steve Rogers are powerful lessons in race and the comic book industry[20, 25].

The 1940s Captain America arrived in the wake of Superman, Batman, and Wonder Woman from the minds and pencil of Joe Simon and Jack Kirby. Uber-patriotic, these foundational stories, including the *original* origin of Steve Rogers' transformation into Captain America, are xenophobic and perversely fueled by eugenics[22]. Somehow the medically altered superhuman maneuvers in the U.S. were morally superior to Hitler's parallel ethnic cleansing. The 1970s Marvel recasting of Captain America by Kirby and Stan Lee reflected the changing social mood about war (Vietnam), and laid the foundation for coming face-to-face with race and civil rights with the addition of Sam Wilson/The Falcon (to be explored in detail below). Although this new Captain America in the Silver Age incorporated the best and worst of Blaxploitation conventions found in films of the era [20, 26], this new origin sought to erase traces of eugenics from the Captain America mythos[22].

From the 1980s (a hot decade for rebooting origins, highlighted by Frank Miller's Batman) and into the early 2000s, Captain

America's origin continued to be reshaped. Notable for a consideration of race is *Truth: Red, White and Black* from 2003, which details a remarkable alternate origin as a medical experiment on black men (echoing Tuskegee), resulting in Isaiah Bradley ascension as the actual first Captain America[20, 22, 23, 27]. While the *Truth/Bradley* side-narrative is important in an investigation of race in comic books, Captain America provides an even more important entry point into race and superhero comic books through the 1970s teaming with Sam Wilson/The Falcon, and then the more recent and new origin story in which Wilson becomes the new (and black) Captain America (see below). However, the entire Captain America mythos, as Hack concludes[22]:

> ... begs the question as to whether comics such as *CA* [Captain America] knowingly presented a different America from the one that actually existed [and exists], or if the creators of these books believed a version of reality in which eugenics was a boon to civic virtue and in which no American would knowingly profit from Nazism. ... Good and evil were [and are] presented in reductionist terms, and offered little of what contemporary conservatives decry as moral relativism; yet these distinctions were no less blurry in pre-war America as they are today: war, as always, is business (p. 88).

It is in that broader context, I believe, that the Falcon and Wilson's donning the cowl of Captain America are central pieces of the complex puzzle revealing how comic books address race.

So Captain America has always been a fascist. But we actually didn't need Marvel's newest reveal to know that.

Captain America has always been *our* fascist, and that is all that matters.

See Also:

Hydra the Beautiful: The American Roots of Captain America's Quasi-Nazi Revelation, Noah Berlatsky

LGBT Visibility: This Fucking Week, Matt Santori-Griffith

Oyola, O. (2015, November 3). The Captain White America Needs [blog]. *The Middle Spaces.*

Whitewashing Muhammad Ali: Our Racist Past, Present, and Future

Throughout my social media connections, in the wake of Muhammad Ali's death, a warning and a prediction were common: do not allow Muhammad Ali to be whitewashed and watch as people whitewash Muhammad Ali.

On ESPN radio, during a show soliciting people to call in about Muhammad Ali, I listened as George Foreman shared an anecdote about Muhammad Ali and Foreman discussing God, reaching the conclusion that Muhammad Ali transcended race.

Muhammad Ali did not transcend race. A black man, he *was* race. He punched racism in its cowardly face.

This whitewashing of Muhammad Ali has a long history, in fact. It is what we do in the U.S. to mask our racist past, to deny our racist present, and to insure our racist future.

In "Muhammad Ali's deification shows an America reluctant

to confront its past," Michael Ezra explained: "[Muhammad Ali's] emergence as boxing's *eminence grise*, one of the country's most beloved figures, tells us much about how Americans construct the past to make sense of the present."

After outlining Muhammad Ali's tumultuous fame and infamy, Ezra concluded about the resurrected and recreated Muhammad Ali: "But Ali's return to glory has come at a price; it is predicated on the whitewashing of his past and the silencing of his voice."

Under the weight of disease and now shrouded in death, Muhammad Ali has been subsumed by the very demon of the U.S. that he chose to fight with dire consequences to himself and his career as a boxer.

Muhammad Ali has been reduced to a caricature to suit white America in the same way Martin Luther King Jr. has been trivialized as a passive radical.

"Transcending race," "post-racial," and "I don't see race" are codes that blind of progressive racism[28], of what Ta-Nehisi Coates calls "elegant racism."

The vilest examples came when Muhammad Ali died and mostly, but not exclusively, right-wing political leaders—who are racists, who court racists, who are xenophobes, who court xenophobes, who are Islamophobic, and who court Islamophobes— offered effusive praise for Muhammad Ali as the Greatest of All Time, quoting his butterfly-and-bee line in the same shallow way white America embraces King's "I have a dream."

Muhammad Ali was far from perfect—being flawed matters only about people with minority statuses in the U.S.—but Muhammad Ali was never Michael Jordan or Tiger Woods, apolitical (as in, the safe sort of whitewashed market "political") Nike pitchmen.

Ask Richard Sherman, Marshawn Lynch, or Colin Kaepernick about being a political black athlete *today*.

Muhammad Ali has to be whitewashed because he did not gain his historical importance from "speaking his mind" (all sorts of blowhards and moral vermin "speak their minds"), but from being on the right side of morality about racism and militarism in the U.S.

If you are uncertain about race and racism in the U.S. right now, and want a peek into how racism will endure into our future, read comments posted online.

Also *right now* you can witness the most insidious forms of whitewashing through the political and media manipulation of inexcusable hate and violence, which Clint Smith confronts in "There Is No Justice in Killing Dylann Roof":

> Last week, the U.S. Department of Justice announced that it would seek the death penalty in the case of Dylann Roof, the twenty-two-year-old accused of walking into the Emanuel A.M.E. Church in Charleston, South Carolina, last year and murdering nine black members of its congregation after spending the preceding hour praying alongside them.

Smith challenges the call for the death penalty, highlighting the support from the political Left and concluding:

> Those who support the death penalty are accepting a practice that is both ineffective and fundamentally flawed. It means supporting a system that not infre-

quently kills those with serious mental illness. It means supporting a system in which an execution is far more likely to take place when the convicted murder is black and the victim is white, than it is when the victim is black and the killer is white. It means supporting a system that has sentenced, and continues to sentence, innocent people to death. In our impulse to rid the world of those we find reprehensible, we forget that we are also ridding the world of those who have done nothing wrong.

Instead, Smith acknowledges:

Roof is not a historical anomaly as much as a representation of a past that America prefers to sweep under its rug rather than commit to cleaning up....Killing Roof does nothing other than soothe the moral conscience of a country that would rather not reckon with the forces that created and cultivated his ideology.

The real and complicated Muhammad Ali offered the U.S. who we could be, but we are dedicated to whitewashing instead.

We remain unable to see that Donald Trump and Dylan Roof are who we have been, who we are, and who we are likely to be—as long as we refuse to see, we refuse to act with the sort of moral conscience that a black Muslim chose instead of playing the game demanded of him.

On Bravado: "He Was Willing to Speak His Mind"

Why did you listen to that man, that man's a balloon
"Friend of Mine," The National

Someday soon, we will be able to look back at 2016 through the more nuanced lens of history, and part of that re-creation must include the recurring praise "He was willing to speak his mind." A coincidence of history, in fact, has brought us this refrain for two men: Donald Trump and the recently deceased Muhammad Ali.

Right-wing apologist and commentator Cal Thomas's "Explaining Donald Trump" has equated Trump and Ali, mostly as an attempt to mask Trump's racism and all-around bigotry as part of his political appeal:

> If there is one explanation for Donald Trump's success it is this: Unlike most Republicans, he fights back. He may not have the late Muhammad Ali's finesse, but he sees himself as more than capable of dealing a "knockout"

punch to Hillary Clinton in November. That ought to be the goal of any GOP presidential nominee.

Even among Ali's most ardent supporters—former combatants in boxing, major sports figures, friends, and relatives—Ali's brashness, bravado is highlighted as a central reason for his greatness (praise that sounds a great deal like why supporters of Trump explain his appeal as a presidential candidate):

> "Ali was one of the first athletes to speak his mind, and that opened the door for the many who do so today. ... He freed us all in that way." The man who sang those praises for Ali was Derek Jeter, the retired Yankee shortstop who never uttered a controversial, or even particularly interesting, statement his entire career. And why would he? His sponsors — Nike, Gatorade, Ford, Movado, Gillette, Visa — would not look kindly on, or write checks to, a rabble-rouser.[29]

In a country where free speech is mostly protected, "speaking one's mind" doesn't really rise to the level of why we should praise anyone.

To be blunt, any fool can speak her/his mind—and Trump is showing us how this can generate great wealth and popularity. Although this is an urgent distinction now, I hope with the passing of time, we can come to see that bravado is not a simple thing.

Trump's bravado is all show; he is a balloon—air puffing up a thin veneer. As a business man—his signature bloviating about *Success!*—he came from wealth and privilege (not self-made, our greatest myth in the U.S.), has run multiple businesses into bankruptcy (a cowardly way to function for such a bully), and would have earned far more money investing instead of his business ventures.

Trump is all *false* bravado. His bluster is irony.

Trump is a shell game best represented by his Trump University. In short, he is the personification of everything that is wrong with capitalism.

Muhammad Ali is the bravado of substance. When he told us he was pretty, he *was* pretty. When he told us he was The Greatest, he *was* The Greatest.

Ali was more genuine, more successful, and more *dignified* in one thirty-minute interview, A Conversation with Muhammad Ali (1968), than Trump has been in his entire cartoon life.

But even at that, Muhammad Ali is not a major figure in human history because of his bravado—not because he was willing to speak his mind.

Again, any fool can do that.

Muhammad Ali is The Greatest because of *what* he said, and the moral stand that he took at great personal sacrifice.

Muhammad Ali was on the right side of racism and militarism (Vietnam specifically) when few others were, and he was willing to take that action even as a significantly marginalized human in a country begrudgingly confronting its *de jure* racism.

Muhammad Ali lived his ethics before himself, and we must not allow his public persona, a purposeful mask of his making, to distract us from his substance.

Trump is all Self(ish), to the detriment of others, any others.

He is a buffoon, as his ridiculous hair, facial gestures, and clown suits *literally* reveal to us.

Bravado is neither inherently good or bad. But we must resist to praise anyone for "speaking her/his mind."

Trump's hollow bravado is an embarrassment to humanity, and it is upon us now to embrace with ample apologies the genuine bravado of Muhammad Ali who never rose to perfection but lived on the right side of history regardless of the costs to his own Self.

The Khan Moment: God, Family, Country

As I learn from you,
I guess you learn from me—
although you're older—and white—
and somewhat more free.
"Theme for English B," Langston Hughes

"'[N]ext to of course god america/ i love you,'" opens e.e. cummings's satirical sonnet about the hollowness of political pandering to love of God, family, country—a staple of stump speeches by both major political parties in the U.S. The speaker turns to war toward the end:

why talk of beauty what could be more beautiful than these heroic happy dead
who rushed like lions to the roaring slaughter
they did not stop to think they died instead ...

Late in the presidential election cycle of 2016, this poem resonated in a way that should leave every American resolute to defend the ideals we claim are at the core of a free people.

As summer crept toward fall, we were not just about to elect a president, but were faced with a test; it was pass/fail and there are no re-takes.

The test was the Khan moment[30], when a grieving Muslim family spoke out at the Democratic National Convention to confront the rising and emboldened bigotry that is personified by Donald Trump but endemic of the Republican Party (see Corey Robin's "Trump's Indecent Proposal").

For decades, the Republican playbook has included a wink-wink-nod-nod approach to very thinly veiled courting of racists, sexists, bigots, and homophobes. Trump took that playbook to a new level—with outright Islamophobia and xenophobia at the center.

Like Pat Tillman, Humayun Khan proudly embraced his service to his country, according to his mother, who was directly slandered by Trump:

> My son Humayun Khan, an Army captain, died 12 years ago in Iraq. He loved America, where we moved when he was 2 years old. He had volunteered to help his country, signing up for the ROTC at the University of Virginia. This was before the attack of Sept. 11, 2001. He didn't have to do this, but he wanted to.[31]

Tillman's and Khan's service and deaths share being politicized for partisan purposes—adding additional layers of insult to injury.

But both also are about far more than partisan politics; they expose that cummings was right: Political pandering to God, family, and country as well as the public's cheering for that pandering is ultimately hollow.

Both Republican and Democrat politicians are warmongers, elites willing to fight wars on the backs of the "heroic happy dead."

The Khan moment, however, raised a blunt question: Which party, which candidate, Trump or Hillary, are racists, sexists, homophobes, Islamophobes, and/or xenophobes supporting?

And there is the damning truth because Trump and the Republican Party are the voices of bigotry.

Many, myself included, believe the war in which Humayun Khan died was yet another senseless war, a waste of human life and valuable national resources.

Many also recognize that the Khan family as well as others scarred by these wars have no political party unsullied by warmongering.

Yet, as a pacifist, I must acknowledge that many marginalized people choose to join, serve, fight, and die in the U.S. military.

Black, brown, gay, female, and Muslim—these soldiers may be guided by higher ideals than the calloused and hollow political leaders waging those wars.

What, then, would these marginalized people be fighting for?

The Khan moment stood before us a test about religious freedom.

A young Muslim man may have seen far more promise for

religious freedom in the U.S. than in other countries—until after his sacrifice his parents had to sit by and listen to Trump call for religious intolerance, to watch as a major political party nominated this man in the wake of naked hatred.

Religious freedom for some, but not others, is not religious freedom.

"Injustice anywhere is a threat to justice everywhere," King warned in his Letter from Birmingham Jail.

The Khan moment was not about limited government, taxation, crumbling infrastructures, or hundreds of legitimate but ultimately mundane issues about which people can have partisan political disagreements.

The Khan moment was about the Statue of Liberty, the Constitution, and the continuing inability of people in the U.S. to *live* the ideals instead of simply mouthing them.

Misogyny 2016

No, this isn't the easy attack on Donald Trump as a misogynist.

In fact, the warranted attacks on Trump's many flaws are often incomplete by omission: Trump's racism, xenophobia, Islamophobia, misogyny, et al., are *ours*.

But the presidential race has exposed misogyny 2016:

- "You Can Be Anti-Trump Without Slut-Shaming Melania," Zeba Blay

- "So what if Malia Obama wants to dance and Melania Trump once posed nude?," Laura Bates

And let us not ignore the misogyny and sexism in how Hillary Clinton is portrayed and vilified. Bates, I believe, sums up the mess perfectly in her closing:

> To tear down wives and daughters as if they are empty vessels of family honour is dangerous and demeaning. But it also distracts us from the real issues. Most political men offer ample opportunities for criticism, all by

themselves.

In many, too many, ways, the Trump monster is the ugly manifestation and reflection of who we are. In our finger pointing, let's recognize how many fingers are turned back at us.

The Eternal Narcissism of White Privilege

The nomination of Donald Trump by the Republican Party spawned a growing body of punditry seeking ways to explain Trump's rise without directly addressing racism, bigotry, and xenophobia.

The explanation *du jour* cautioned critics of Trump supporters, arguing that Trump is attractive to working-class whites who have legitimate fears. Works such as *Hillbilly Elegy* by J.D. Vance have become representative of the serious reconsideration of the angry white voter, as Vance proclaims:

> The simple answer is that these people–my people–are really struggling, and there hasn't been a single political candidate who speaks to those struggles in a long time. Donald Trump at least tries.[32]

However, as a redneck son of the self-defeating South, I immediately had a different reaction to Vance and the scramble to attend to the eternal narcissism of white privilege: In *The Eternal Sunshine of the Spotless Mind*, the four-year-old Joel frets about his mother: "She's not looking at me. No one ever looks at me."

The histrionics of working class whites, to me, sound like arrested development, spurred by the long deferred political and social recognition about racism prompted by the #BlackLivesMatter movement.

The consequences of white privilege include that privilege is *both* ever-present *and* thus invisible—much as we say that fish don't understand water.

And thus, while working-class whites have suffered because of disaster capitalism and the vast majority of the policies implemented by the Republican machine they support, the narcissism of privilege among working-class whites in the U.S. blinds them from two powerful and damning facts:

1. **White privilege buoys all whites** in comparison to black and brown people in terms of socioeconomic opportunity and wealth as well as shielding whites from the negative consequences of the U.S. judicial system and policing. Just as two examples, whites who dropped out of high school have the same employment opportunities as blacks with some college, and blacks constitute only about 12% of the U.S. population, but mass incarceration impacts 2207/100,000 blacks compared to 380/100,000 whites.

2. **Working-class whites have supported Republicans for ideological reasons linked to religious and racial bigotry**—while disregarding how that commitment has been self-defeating to their own interests. As Neil Gross explains

in "The Decline of Unions and the Rise of Trump": "Union decline [*as a subset of many economic factors, I want to add*] has left the [white] working class politically and economically vulnerable, and it's this vulnerability Mr. Trump has been able to exploit."

This "O, crap!" moment for working-class whites isn't without merit, but it comes with the same sort of false logic found in the South where whites shout for blacks to "Get over slavery" while clutching and waving the Confederate battle flag and screaming "Tradition!"

Again, as a life-long Southerner, I am compelled despite my own skepticism about organized religion, especially the fundamentalist kind of my home region, to proclaim that working-class whites need to have a Come-to-Jesus moment.

First, while recognizing the power of white privilege regardless of socioeconomic status is essential, working-class whites must *forefront* the concerns of black and brown people who suffer disproportionately for the mere fact of their race in the U.S.

Next, working-class whites must form a solidarity with all people who share their social and economic needs: *working-class status* is more significant for equity in the U.S. than religious or racial differences.

And finally, working-class whites must reject the "Make American Great Again" mantra since there is no compelling evidence to support either that the U.S. was once great or that somehow the expansion of freedom and equity beyond whiteness is anti-American.

Again, in a blazing display of illogic, while working-class

whites remain committed to mythologies such as "a rising tide lifts all boats," they have politically resisted expanding—and ideologically refuse even to acknowledge these inequities exist or matter—marriage rights to homosexuals, social and economic equity to black and brown Americans, equal pay for women, American citizenship for immigrants, the end to mass incarceration for recreational marijuana use—all of which raises the tide for everyone in the U.S. by growing freedom.

If we concede to the mainstream whitewashing of Trump and his supporters; if we continue not to name bigotry, racism, and xenophobia; if we only attend to anything once it becomes a white problem—we are failing the very thing the Right and conservatives are so quick to shout about: life, liberty, and the pursuit of happiness.

The "yes, but" narcissism of white privilege once again is shouting over #BlackLivesMatter, and their ring-leader is the king of shouting over substance.

Working-class whites need to put on their grown-up pants, sit down, listen patiently, and *wait their turn*—finally.

Bizarro Politics and Fearing the "Other"

For decades, I was wasting my votes in South Carolina by aggressively voting against Republicans. I really never voted *for* a Democrat, but I certainly found all the Republicans so vile that I felt a moral duty to vote against them.

Then in 2005, I was sitting in a hotel in New Orleans just months before Katrina hit and watching an interview on TV with George Carlin. Prompted by Charlie Rose about the 1992 election, Carlin explained that he was a lifelong non-voter.

Since then, like W.E.B. Du Bois and Carlin, I have been a non-voter and very openly *not* a Republican, Democrat, or (the silliest of all) Independent.

With the rise of Trump, I also resisted addressing this new and unprecedented level of insanity in mainstream politics: Trump is a bizarro cartoon extreme of everything wrong with partisan politics and the U.S. (although he certainly isn't an extreme conservative, which I address below).

Recently, I have broken my Golden Rule of not mentioning the fools who live by the glory of being mentioned, even when being called fools (again, Trump is the king of that foolishness).

I also have been forced to reconsider partisan politics—most disturbingly, to acknowledge that if the Republicans had nominated Jeb Bush, they would have had a very powerful leg to stand on in terms of refuting Hillary Clinton over ethics and honesty.

Yes, we all could have quibbled over policy (I detest Jeb Bush's policy, especially the dumpster fire of education policy in Florida), but Jeb Bush proved himself one of the most honest candidates in the primary campaign, and Hillary Clinton has a legitimate credibility problem (one that is typical of almost all candidates and only easily exposed by an unusually ethical, honest candidate).

And while there is a long and disturbing history (especially in the South) of major blocks of voters voting against their best interests, the Trump phenomenon, again, is a truly extreme example of that paradox.

I have begun to understand this better after seeing a photo with a news story about Trump: A line of young white males all wearing "build the wall" t shirts mimicking Pink Floyd's *The Wall* (possibly in the top three most offensive things I have seen in the campaign as a Pink Floyd fan).

Trump has risen along a continuum of Republicans who have maintained the religious right's support despite multiple infidelities and divorces, as well as amassing wealth that clearly contradicts the whole camel through an eye of a needle idea of reaching heaven.

Trump also has seemingly increased the loyalty of poor and working class whites—despite his being the sort of business man who has exploited and ignored those populations to amass and squander his wealth. (We worship the wealthy in the U.S. and conveniently ignore that wealth is always built on the backs of workers who are left out of that wealth loop.)

I don't want to catalogue the many contradictions between who Trump is and those subgroups who support him, but it is without question that Trump maintains support from many stake-holders who are somehow putting aside that *he does not represent them* in order to remain rabidly behind him.

Along with the "my team" aspect of partisan politics in the U.S. (a certain number of Republicans and Democrats, for example, would vote for anyone on their "team," even if we simply swapped candidates), I believe there is one extremely disturbing common denominator cementing the Trump wall: fearing the "other."

Trump has garnered the support of the anti-government Republican party with mantras of "I can do this for you" and with plans such as the federal government building a wall between Mexico and the U.S. (huge time and tax money commitments from the "less government" crowd?).

The "build the wall" refrain of the Trump campaign is simul-taneously the most *irrational* and most compelling and solidifying aspect of his run.

Then the Newt Gingrich moment[33] when he refused to acknowledge violent crime is down in the U.S. by insisting that it is more important that the public *believes* there is more crime—this is the "wall" element writ large.

Trump is the orange-faced, wild-haired Clown Leader of Fear—a very bad script plagiarized from a much better Stephen King novel.

The fear of the "other" feeds Islamophobia, racism, sexism/misogyny, homophobia, etc., and can be maintained only through ignorance and delusion.

And mainstream cloaked-racist refrains such as "black-on-black crime" have created the foundation upon which the Trump Circus has been built.

Some continue to argue that we must not demonize Trump supporters as stupid, but I believe that reasonable call is deeply flawed.

Do poor and working class whites have reason to be disillusioned? Of course, but that doesn't excuse their misinformed responses.

White high school drop outs have the same employment opportunities as blacks with some college (see *Closing the Race Gap*, Rory O'Sullivan, Konrad Mugglestone, and Tom Allison), but the angry poor/working class voters supporting Trump will not admit their white privilege, and refuse to address the complicated facts of a racist U.S. society.

So the ultimate paradox of the rise of Heir Clown Trump is that "build the wall" is the real unifying theme that discredits his "Make America Great Again"—because, if we were informed at all, we may be compelled to see just what our country's values are regarding the "other":

The New Colossus

Not like the brazen giant of Greek fame,
With conquering limbs astride from land to land;
Here at our sea-washed, sunset gates shall stand
A mighty woman with a torch, whose flame
Is the imprisoned lightning, and her name
Mother of Exiles. From her beacon-hand

Glows world-wide welcome; her mild eyes command
The air-bridged harbor that twin cities frame.
"Keep ancient lands, your storied pomp!" cries she
With silent lips. "Give me your tired, your poor,
Your huddled masses yearning to breathe free,
The wretched refuse of your teeming shore.
Send these, the homeless, tempest-tost to me,
I lift my lamp beside the golden door!"

Listening to Langston Hughes about "Make America Great Again"

When an individual is protesting society's refusal to
acknowledge his dignity as a human being, his very act
of protest confers dignity on him.
Bayard Rustin

It's called the American Dream because you have to be
asleep to believe it.
George Carlin

When I met with my first-year writing seminar, Reconsidering James Baldwin in the Era of #BlackLivesMatter, one Monday during the fall of 2016, I noted that the weekend had provided for us local and national examples of why the course matters: locally, one high school restricted students from having U.S. flags at a football game because of patterns of using that flag to taunt and harass rival students who are Latinx/Hispanic, and nationally, Colin Kaepernick was questioned about his sitting during the National Anthem at the beginning of NFL preseason games.

As entry points into the work of Baldwin as well as the long history of racism in the twentieth and twenty-first centuries, I read aloud and we discussed Langston Hughes's "Theme for English B" and "Let America Be America Again."

I stressed to these first-year college students that Hughes lived and wrote in the early to mid-1900s—nearly a *century ago* in terms of the college student personae in "Theme for English B."

As we examined the professor/student and race-based aspects of power in "Theme," students were quick to address the relevance of Hughes today—emphasizing as well part of my instructional purpose to expose these students to the lingering and historical racism in the U.S.

But the real meat of this class session revealed itself as we explored "Let America Be America Again."

Hughes: "(America never was America to me.)"

Written and published about 80 years ago, "Let America Be America Again" represents a racialized dismantling of the American Dream myth—a poetic companion to the skepticism and cynicism of F. Scott Fitzgerald, Ernest Hemingway, and other writers'/artists' works throughout the early to mid-twentieth century.

Hughes begins with a celebratory stanza that easily lulls readers into an uncritical response to the American Dream, but then offers a brilliant device, the use of parentheses, to interject a minority voice (parenthetical, thus representing the muted voices of the marginalized in the U.S.) after several opening stanzas:

(America never was America to me.)...

(It never was America to me.)...

(There's never been equality for me,
Nor freedom in this "homeland of the free.")

And then the poem turns on two italicized lines followed by:

I am the poor white, fooled and pushed apart,
I am the Negro bearing slavery's scars.
I am the red man driven from the land,
I am the immigrant clutching the hope I seek—
And finding only the same old stupid plan
Of dog eat dog, of mighty crush the weak.

My students soon recognized a disturbing paradox: Hughes and Donald Trump's "Make America Great Again" campaign slogan share a foundational claim but for starkly *different* reasons.

Trump has built political capital on anti-immigrant and anti-Muslim (both as "Others") sentiment that the media and pundits often mask behind what is being called legitimate white working-class angst.

Parallel racist anger has been sparked when Michelle Obama, for example, confronted that the White House was built in part with slave labor—raising the issue of just *who* did build this country. *Upon whose backs?* we must ask.

Eight volatile decades ago, Hughes named "the poor white,

fooled and pushed apart" now courted by Trump's coded and blatant racism and xenophobia.

However, Hughes's poem celebrates the diverse workers who created the U.S. while reaping very little if any of the benefits. Hughes offers a different coded assault, his on capitalism and the ruling elites, but not the rainbow of U.S. workers "fooled," it seems, by the hollow promise of the American Dream.

In Whitmanesque style, Hughes raises throughout the poem a collective voice of immigrants and slaves as the foundation of the U.S.:

I'm the man who sailed those early seas
In search of what I meant to be my home—
For I'm the one who left dark Ireland's shore,
And Poland's plain, and England's grassy lea,
And torn from Black Africa's strand I came
To build a "homeland of the free."

But as he returns to the poem's refrain, Hughes unmasks the promise and tempers the hope:

O, let America be America again—
The land that never has been yet—
And yet must be—the land where *every* man is free.

In the final stanza, there is hope, built on "We, the people, must redeem."

In a time of Trump's cartoonish stereotype of the empty politician, his "Build a Wall" and "Make America Great Again" sloganism, we must reach back almost a century to Hughes's often ignored voice that merges races through our shared workers' remorse.

Hughes calls out the robber baron tradition of U.S. capital-ism—"those who live like leeches on the people's lives"—as the "fooled and pushed apart" line up to support those very leeches.

"Let America Be America Again" is a warning long ignored, but truths nonetheless facing us. Silence and inaction are endorse-ments of these truths.

"To be afraid," Bayard Rustin acknowledged in "The Meaning of Birmingham" (1963), "is to behave as if the truth were not true."

It remains to be seen if we are brave enough as a people to "Let America Be America Again."

Arrogance: Service, Not Saviors

Beyond the obvious—that they are all joined by the field of education—what links the National Reading Panel (NRP) and No Child Left Behind, the edureform documentary propaganda *Waiting for "Superman,"* Teach For America, and edusavior Steve Perry?

Arrogance.

While I count myself among English language arts (ELA) teachers who are skeptical of the Great Books mindset—that we have essential books all children must read—I am moved today to endorse how many of those works remind we puny humans about the folly of pride. Not the "I am proud of you daughter/son" pride, but the arrogance pride.

The "'My name is Ozymandias, King of Kings;/ Look on my Works, ye Mighty, and despair!'" kind of pride.

What on earth possessed politicians to form the NRP to find out what we know about teaching children to read? Did anyone point out that we have had a vibrant field of literacy in the U.S. for a good century? Isn't it sort of obvious that we have dozens upon dozens of people across the U.S. who know exactly how to teach children to read (and have known for decades)?

But it isn't just the teaching of reading.

Naive experts, often journalists, every week roll out yet another book in which she or he researches a field in which real experts in that field have been doing authentic work for decades— the history of teaching!, how to teach poor children!, the glory of 10,000 hours of practice!

Paternalistic, self-important, blowhard politicians daily puff up in front of the public to be that "Superman" at the center of the great lie documentary noted above that ironically serves as a perfect representation of *everything that is wrong with education reform.*

But one need not go back to that complete failure of film making.

Educators and activists Andre Perry and Jose Vilson have assumed the mantle of speaking truth to the cult of personality that is Steve Perry.

I consider myself a student of Andre Perry and Vilson, as I work to navigate my own white male privilege in a way that serves others—specifically those marginalized by race and class.

I am a product of white privilege and colonialism, and therefore, must not serve those corrosive forces.

Here, I urge you to read Andre Perry and Vilson, but also to act upon their messages.

And I want to offer a tentative framing informed by their charges.

First, I am compelled by the 30 for 30 series on O.J. Simpson to suggest that Simpson himself is a cautionary tale about the dangers of white privilege and the costs of whitewashing blacks in order for them to be *allowed* into mainstream society.

Next, I find troubling parallels in the work of Steve Perry with powerful blacks (Bill Cosby, Clarence Thomas, and Simpson) who negotiate the whitewashing in their favor at the expense of all other people of color.

The demonizing of dreadlocks, the finger-pointing at sagging pants, the judgmental finger-wagging at black English—yes, these are the tools of white privilege, but they also serve the cult of personality unmasked in Steve Perry, for example, by Andre Perry and Vilson.

Finally, although specific people have to be addressed when confronting the cult of personality, the problem is that those people are serving larger forces that are driving education reform, a movement that uses "civil rights" as a mask to implement policies that are perpetuating colonialism and whitewashing.

"No excuses" charter schools committed to "grit" are about "fixing" black, brown, and poor children.

Zero tolerance policies and grade retention policies disproportionately turn black, brown, and poor children into criminals and drop-outs.

High-stakes testing and accountability produce and perpetuate so-called achievement gaps among race and social class—as well as gate-keep in order to keep "other people's children" in their place.

Teach For America fuels the historical inequity of access to experienced and certified teachers (see Rebecca Klein's "White Students Get Experienced Teachers, While Black Students Get Police In School").

Whether the face of education reform is Bill Gates, Michelle Rhee, Arne Duncan, Geoffrey Canada, or Steve Perry (or the long list of celebrities who decide education is their hobby), and while we must necessarily confront each person as we confront what they represent, the ultimate challenge in rejecting edureform while also calling for building public education as a vehicle for equity and liberation is to call colonialism "colonialism," to just say no to policies and practices designed to erase who children are so that they can be assimilated into society.

There are profound and significant differences in Andre Perry's work, Vilson's daily classroom teaching, and Steve Perry's bloviating (think Donald Trump).

Andre Perry, Vilson, and Chris Emdin, for example, celebrate black students, their humanity as *inseparable* from their blackness—while Steve Perry celebrates Steve Perry (again, think Trump) as one who erases the black from children in the service of white privilege.

We are way past time to stop believing in and listening to these false idols, self-proclaimed "Super(wo)men."

Ozymandias, please recall, was a fool in king's clothing whose words mocked him:

Nothing beside remains. Round the decay
Of that colossal Wreck, boundless and bare
The lone and level sands stretch far away.

Let's not form any more panels, let's not crown any more edusaviors, let's not print and/or buy any more bestselling books by educelebrities (who have never been teachers), let's not worship at the altar of hollow Ted Talks.

Just as we didn't need the NRP to "know how to teach children to read," we have ample knowledge right now how to eradicate racism and classism in our society and our schools.

Edureformers, edusaviors, and educelebrities are in the service of keeping us from that vital work. As Andre Perry asserts in "Black Aesthetic, White Supremacy: Steve Perry's Tweet Needs Cutting More Than Black Boys' Hair":

> Let's be clear: Belt wearing isn't the reason white children are educated in wealthier schools. Haircuts and etiquette classes don't lead to the technological innovations of Silicon Valley. Lower incarceration rates aren't because whites use drugs less often. The wage gap isn't caused by white men's hard work ethic.

But social and educational inequity is the consequence of white privilege. So I ask now that you listen to carefully and then act upon Chris Emdin's confrontation of edureform as colonialism and what choices lie before teachers[34]:

> What I am suggesting is that it is possible for people of all racial and ethnic backgrounds to take on approaches to teaching that hurt youth of color....

I argue that there must be a concerted effort...to challenge the "white folks' pedagogy" that is being practiced by teachers of all ethnic and racial backgrounds....

The time will always come when teachers must ask themselves if they will follow the mold or blaze a new trail. There are serious risks that come with this decision. It essentially boils down to *whether one chooses to do damage to the system or to the student* [emphasis added]. (pp. viii-ix, 206)

Especially in our schools, and especially among our most vulnerable students, we need service, not saviors.

Deplorables Unmasked

Something deplorable happened on the way to claiming the U.S. is a Christian nation of free people where everyone regardless of race, creed, religion, or gender has the same opportunities at life, liberty, and the pursuit of happiness.

And it wasn't Donald Trump. Or better expressed, it wasn't *only* Donald Trump.

Once Trump secured the nomination for president of the Republican Party, many scrambled to caution about condemning Trump's supporters, not painting them with too broad and negative a brush.

Especially in the mainstream media, few, nearly none, would venture to utter words such as "racist," "sexist," "xenophobe," or even "lie."

Trump and his running mate have skated along literally piling lies on top of lies—including lies about not saying provable things, including Trump opening an apology with lies.

But what is truly deplorable is Trump both represents and

has unmasked the ugly truth about the U.S.: we are a nation of deplorables, not as outliers, but as a substantial population of our country.

As I was driving down I-85 in South Carolina on the morning after the suddenly shocking recording of Trump being exactly who he has always been, I saw a large, black SUV in front of me with this bumper sticker:

It has become conventional wisdom to brush off Trump's obnoxious bravado as part of his reality show persona, while adding that his supporters are more nuanced in their support for his candidacy.

But the harsh truth is that Trump is deplorable and so are his supporters—and so are many so-called decent Americans.

Clichés become clichés often because they are true, and one truism seems quite important at this moment: when someone shows you who they really are, be sure to pay attention.

And people often reveal who they really are when they think they are in private, when they think they are among their own kind.

Men hanging out with other men often sound like the Trump comments being rebuked now as if this isn't common language and attitudes.

Having been born, grown up, and now living in the South, I can assure you when whites are in seemingly safe environs, the racism rears its ugly head in subtle and blunt ways.

But it is even worse than that.

When we experienced yet more evidence of who Trump is, who his enablers are, the carefully prepared political backpedaling told us just as much as any hot mic:

> "I am sickened by what I heard today," [Paul] Ryan said through a spokesman, about five hours after The Washington Post published a 2005 recording of Trump boasting of groping women and trying to have sex with a married woman. "Women are to be championed and revered, not objectified. I hope Mr. Trump treats this situation with the seriousness it deserves and works to demonstrate to the country that he has greater respect for women than this clip suggests."[35]

Gross, pig sexist being chastised by his more well-groomed but equally clueless sexist—as part and parcel of who the Republican Party has always been, as part and parcel of who many in the U.S. remain to be via Twitter:

Susan Schorn @SusanSchorn

"'Women are to be championed and revered, not objectified,' Ryan said."

Dude. "Championing" and "revering" ARE objectifying. #evolve

When Trump vilified Mexicans and Muslims, when Trump repeatedly stirs racism and caters to openly racist groups, the mainstream political response remains trapped in respecting human dignity only by close association—such as the hot take in the mainstream press to speak with reverence about mothers and daughters.

A people has no moral compass, no ethical grounding if the only way anyone can respect human dignity is by association.

If you have to know or be related to people with other statuses than yours to care about their human dignity, you are deplorable.

Some may now try to burn at the stake the Frankenstein's monster, Donald Trump, but to do so without acknowledging Dr. Frankenstein is misguided and shallow political theater.

Trump as bogus billionaire entrepreneur, as con-man reality star is the white male prototype of what it means to be an American: America built this.

And, as much as we wish to deny it, we are America.

The America who tells Colin Kaepernick not to sully our sacred football with politics—while failing to see that opening every football game with the National Anthem *is political*.

The America who responds to #BlackLivesMatter with All Lives Matter—while refusing to admit that guns matter more than any lives.

The America that polices how some people raise their fists—while "land of the free and home of the brave" proves to be false on both counts.

Something deplorable happened on the way to claiming the U.S. is a Christian nation of free people where everyone regardless of race, creed, religion, or gender has the same opportunities at life, liberty, and the pursuit of happiness.

Something deplorable is right there in the mirror.

It's Just How Men Talk— And That's the Problem

In the friendly banter scene from *Notting Hill*, several men are sitting at a restaurant having a lewd and boisterous conversation about Meg Ryan and then Anna Scott, the fictional world-famous actress featured in the romantic comedy and who coincidentally is sitting out of sight but nearby with William Thacker.

The scene is intended to match the mostly humorous but semi-critical subtext of the film about the pressures of being a celebrated actress in Hollywood: being famous isn't all it's cracked up to be, especially if you are a woman.

However, the scene isn't funny at all, but it is a reflection of how men talk—of the normalized culture all Western men have been *raised in* and *tolerate* and/or *participate in*, which is the male gaze[36] and the objectifying discourse that is an extension of the male gaze.

This allowed Donald Trump to brush off his 1995 hot-mic bragging about physical and sexual assault (we have no way to know if he is exaggerating, but he has never disavowed his story) as "locker room talk"—it's just how men talk.

However, like much of the 2016 presidential campaign, allowing this excuse is yet more false equivalence.

Trump's language and the behavior it represents are rape culture[37], not merely objectifying discourse from the male gaze.

This distinction proves to be as unsatisfying as the false equivalence because the *male gaze/objectifying discourse as normal is the context within which rape culture thrives.*

Many men sit just as the men in the *Notting Hill* scene do— with a jovial tone no less—sexualizing women, especially women who are famous, and women who dress in a way that men have deemed sexual.

The male gaze and the objectifying discourse grounded in that gaze probably rarely extends to assault—but even among men who consider themselves good people, many men, if not most men, have also coerced sex with women they considered just an opportunity for sport sex, a one-night stand, and even with significant others, lovers, and spouses.

And even among men who consider themselves good people, many men, if not most men, have also made women feel uncomfortable, threatened, because all women live with the prevalent awareness of not only the male gaze but the capacity for male physical and sexual aggression.

And thus, it is a real but ultimately pointless line between "friendly banter" (male gaze, objectifying discourse) and rape culture because it isn't a line; rape culture is a very real and very horrible subset of friendly banter.

As in all situations within which some have power over others, it is the responsibility of men to confront and end both the male gaze/objectifying discourse and rape culture.

Those men who participate cavalierly in the male gaze and "friendly banter"—most if not all men—have an urgent responsibility to name and reject the uglier rape culture represented with disgusting glee by Trump and by serial celebrity rapists such as Bill Cosby.

But men must also begin to disassemble the falsely characterized "friendly banter" culture as well.

It is entirely valid for those men who believe themselves to be good men to claim they are not Trump, his bravado and predatory behavior are not them, and to admit their own culpability in the culture that has bred and allowed Trump and other predatory men to exist.

Trump's language and predatory behavior—that is not just how men talk and act, but in the grand scheme of things, that distinction really doesn't matter because how men talk does create a world in which women's lives too often do not matter beyond their being objectified, sexualized, and reduced to their relationship statuses.

Most men, I hope, do not want *to be* or be considered a monster, a predator. Trump has outed himself as a predator, a part of rape culture, an active and cavalier aggressor.

Among many other examples, these facts of his true self disqualify him for being a serious candidate for any credible position in society.

Men must and can distance themselves from rape culture, but that must not be used as a shield for the many ways in which men are uncritical and unconscious participants in the male gaze and "friendly banter."

Yes, it is urgent for everyone to reject rape culture, and the newest face on that, Trump, but it is well past time to admit that the male gaze and objectifying discourse strip women of their human dignity and sully every man's humanity as well.

See Also:

Emily Ratajkowski: Baby Woman

Republicans Have a Yuge Logic Problem

The new (and disgusting) face of the Republican Party, Donald Trump, anchored his campaign on a foundational slogan he "inherited" from Ronald Reagan[38] (like the millions he squandered from his father): Make America Great Again.

Setting aside that Trump is either a liar (well, is a liar) or is incredibly stupid since he claims he created that slogan, the concept itself creates a *yuge* logic problem for the Republican Party.

First, the slogan directly states America is now *not great*.

If this is true, it certainly reads next that whoever is running our state and federal governments must be at least significantly to blame for the lack of greatness, right?

Among Republicans, the anti-government roar has a long and loud history.

So here comes the logic problem: In 2017, Republicans control the vast majority of state and federal power in the U.S.

That means that if America is now not great, and if government is to blame, then the Republican Party and its candidates are the source of all this not-greatness.

Thus, how in the hell was it logical to vote for Trump or any Republicans?

Hint: It wasn't.

Disclaimer:

I am not now a Democrat, and I have never been a member of any political party. I did not support Hillary Clinton. I very openly campaigned against anyone voting for Trump because he is uniquely a horrible human and candidate. A reasonable person could argue for Hillary or a third party candidate, but nothing could justify supporting Trump.

Harrison Bergeron 2016

Along with *Slaughterhouse-Five*, Kurt Vonnegut's short story "Harrison Bergeron" is one of his most taught, and thus most read, works. Both narratives also represent Vonnegut's characteristic genre bending and blending—notably dark satire with science fiction.

"Harrison Bergeron" is the second story in Kurt Vonnegut's iconic *Welcome to the Monkey House* collection of short stories. However, as I have examined[39], "Harrison Bergeron" is often misread and misinterpreted, reflected in the film adaptation *2081*.

In 2016-2017, how and why the story is misread and misinterpreted—forcing on it American faith in the rugged individual and refusing to acknowledge Vonnegut's principles grounded in socialism and free thinking—is a powerful commentary on U.S. politics broadly and Donald Trump specifically.

Misreading, Misinterpreting "Harrison Bergeron"

Vonnegut's fiction and nonfiction are anything except simple—

even though he practices a style that can be called "simple" because of his accessible vocabulary, mostly brief and simple sentence structure, and staccato paragraphing (which he claimed mimics the structure of jokes).

Yet, many impose onto "Harrison Bergeron" a simplistic theme (anti-communism) and a simplistic reading of Harrison as hero.

"If 'Harrison Bergeron' is a satire against the Left," however, as Darryl Hattenhauer details[40], "then it is inconsistent with the rest of Vonnegut's fiction."

The misinterpretation stems from expecting narratives to have heroes and from careless reading of what the story says about equality; Hattenhauer clarifies:

> But the object of Vonnegut's satire is not all leveling—
> "any leveling process" that might arise. Rather, the object
> of his satire is the popular misunderstanding of what
> leveling and equality entail. More specifically, this text
> satirizes America's Cold War misunderstanding of not
> just communism but also socialism.

Vonnegut's enduring real-life hero was Eugene V. Debs, possibly the most well-known and influential socialist in U.S. history. Vonnegut was a lifelong advocate for socialism, and "Vonnegut's concern for the working class eventually blossomed into a full-scale political outlook that was inspired by a combination of Midwestern populism and home-grown American socialism," explains Matthew Gannon and Wilson Taylor[41].

Yet, the short film *2081* adapts "Harrison Bergeron" painstakingly true to Vonnegut—except for almost entirely missing that the story itself satirizes *both* the totalitarian state (embodied by Handicapper General Diana Moon Glampers) with its militaristic police force *and* Harrison Bergeron as megalomaniac would-be "Emperor!"

Again, as Hattenhauer emphasizes: "Like his fiction, Vonnegut's non-fiction also satirizes the Right and endorses the Left. And the Left it endorses is not liberalism (America is one of the few nations where liberalism is not centrist)."

Therefore, "Harrison Bergeron" defies both being simple and America's cartoonish hatred of communism as *forced equality* (a cultural failure to distinguish between brute *equality* and social *equity*). The story, Hattenhauer examines, has an unreliable narration, which describes a dystopian totalitarian state in which "anti-intellectual leveling" is satirized—not "income redistribution," which Vonnegut as socialist endorsed.

Vonnegut attacks, then, the exact American myths that many who misread the story claim it endorses, as detailed by Hattenhauer:

> According to the proponents of the ideology of America's dominant culture, equal income redistribution would contradict the fact that some are smarter than others (the corollary: the rich are smart and the poor are dumb), and also contradict the fact that some are better looking or more athletic than others (the corollary: attractive and athletic people deserve wealth).

Nonetheless, "Harrison Bergeron," understood as Vonnegut intended, proves to be a powerful commentary on the 2016 presidential election and the rise of Donald Trump.

Harrison Bergeron 2016

Vonnegut's writing never fits neatly into clear genre categories, but like Margaret Atwood, he constantly plays with and within genre conventions both in loving devotion to the forms and in ways that defy those conventions.

As well, Vonnegut's fiction resists traditional portrayals of the hero and main characters. Billy Pilgrim and Harrison Bergeron, for example, are not heroes—but they are not anti-heroes or every-man main characters.

In many ways, Vonnegut keeps an even focus on many characters throughout his works, and tends to include a mixture of positive and negative qualities in even the most static characters—mostly because nearly everything and everyone in Vonnegut is open to satire.

Charles Shields and Gregory Sumner suggest Vonnegut is nearly always the main character in his work, as authorial voice overseeing even identified narrators.

As a result, Harrison Bergeron is presented through an unreliable narrator as larger than life; at 14 years old, Harrison is seven feet tall and "a genius." But the reader soon learns, as a fugitive, "Harrison's appearance was Halloween and hardware."

In short, Vonnegut's dystopia and Harrison as a character are *cartoonish*.

"Clanking, clownish, and huge" as well as "wear[ing] at all times a red rubber ball for a nose," Harrison bursts into the story with "'I am the Emperor!'"

Misread as rugged individual hero, Harrison is, in fact, a megalomaniac—his bombast a sour joke.

Yet, as a *genius* and a renegade, he remains a threat to the totalitarian state; thus:

> It was then that Diana Moon Glampers, the Handicapper General, came into the studio with a double-barreled ten-gauge shotgun. She fired twice, and the Emperor and the Empress were dead before they hit the floor.

Vonnegut's dark, dark cartoon of a story ends with a joke worthy of a drumroll, but the story cannot be read with a smile in 2017 because Harrison Bergeron has been manifest in reality as Republican president, Donald Trump.

Trump as faux-billionaire, bombastic failed business man, and reality TV star stands before the U.S. as a threat as well—although to the promise (albeit tarnished) of democracy.

Enough Americans misread Trump as a hero to suggest why so many misread "Harrison Bergeron" as some sort of anti-communist propaganda: our rose-colored rugged individualism lenses are powerful, like the "spectacles with thick wavy lenses" worn by Harrison "to make him not only half blind, but to give him whanging headaches besides."

The flaw in the American character that makes so many misread Trump is not simple either. Yes, there is racism and misogyny—but there is also a profound tension between a *valid fear of totalitarianism* and a simple-minded blurring of communism/socialism with totalitarianism.

When government *actually is* indistinguishable from the military (Diana Moon Glampers), a people have lost their precious freedom.

But Vonnegut's cartoon dystopia omits entirely the utopian possibility of democratic socialism and free thinking that Vonnegut championed his entire life—and that many, if not most, in the U.S. remain unable to embrace.

"Harrison Bergeron" does speak to the center-right politics of the U.S., in which the so-called left is represented by a classic Republican (Hillary Clinton) and the so-called right has been reduced to a clown (Trump).

If this were a Vonnegut story or novel, it would be goddam funny.

As real life, the presidential election of 2016 is a metaphorical "double-barreled ten-gauge shotgun" aimed at our heads, and it is in our hands with our fingers on the trigger.

"History proves that the white man is a devil"

The public career and life of Malcolm X are fraught with contradictions and controversy—often complicated by the Nation of Islam and its discredited leader Elijah Muhammad.

Malcolm X's infamy—as it contrasts with the idealizing and misrepresentation of Martin Luther King Jr. as a passive radical—lies often in his sloganized "By any means necessary" and "History proves that the white man is a devil."

While Malcolm X himself confronted some of his more controversial and confrontational stances, in 2016, the U.S. is faced with the prescience in what seemed to be hyperbole and racial anger; however, there is much to consider about the evil capacity often behind the face of white men.

Living just across the highways from my neighborhood, Todd Kohlhepp[42] has confessed to vicious murders after police found a woman chained in a storage container for two months.

Kohlhepp represents to a disturbing degree the classic profile of serial killers and sex offenders, central of which is being a white male. At the University of Wisconsin:

> The 20-year-old student, Alec Cook, has been arrested and appeared in court on Thursday, charged with 15 crimes against five women, including sexual assault, strangulation and false imprisonment. His modus operandi, according to police and prosecutors, was to befriend fellow students and eventually entrap and viciously attack them, while keeping notebooks detailing his alleged targets.[43]

Kohlhepp and Cook, white males of relative affluence, are no outliers. Yet, political leaders and the media persist in characterizing for the U.S. public much different images of who to fear: Mexicans, black males, Muslims.

Daily violence—including sexual aggression and assault—is a real threat in a way nearly opposite of these political and media messages; each of us should fear people who look like us, and family, friends, and acquaintances deserve nearly equal scrutiny.

Political race-baiters and the mainstream media rarely stray from the black-on-black crime message, but also always fail to add a key fact: crime is almost entirely intra-racial as the white-on-white crime rate (86%) is nearly identical to the black-on-black crime rate (94%).

Malcolm X's rhetoric may still seem inflammatory, but James Baldwin's more measured charges confront the same racial masking and tension:

> White Americans find it as difficult as white people elsewhere do to divest themselves of the notion that they are

in possession of some intrinsic value that black people need, or want. And this assumption—which, for example, makes the solution to the Negro problem depend on the speed with which Negroes accept and adopt white standards—is revealed in all kinds of striking ways, from Bobby Kennedy's assurance that a Negro can become President in forty years to the unfortunate tone of warm congratulation with which so many liberals address their Negro equals. It is the Negro, of course, who is presumed to have become equal—an achievement that not only proves the comforting fact that perseverance has no color but also overwhelmingly corroborates the white man's sense of his own value.[44]

White men control the political and media narratives, and thus, white males are bathed in the compassionate light of the white male gaze of power—everyone else becomes the feared Other.

The hatred spewed by Donald Trump is not solely what should be feared in this context, but that he personifies and speaks to "the white man's sense of his own value" that seeks to erase that Other, as Astra Taylor reported in "Thursday in Selma, North Carolina" from a Trump rally:

A few months ago Trump had rallied in Wilmington, North Carolina, the site of America's only and largely forgotten coup. In 1898, in the waning days of Reconstruction, rioting white supremacists overthrew a multiracial progressive "fusion" government, deposing democratically elected leaders of both races and killing black citizens mercilessly. After that, populism in North Carolina, as in the South more broadly, was a white affair. At his rally near the site of that historic, shocking savagery, Trump suggested "the Second Amendment people" do something about Hillary.

The Trump narrative is essentially racist, and almost entirely false; Jason Stanley's "Beyond Lying: Donald Trump's Authoritarian Reality" explains:

> The chief authoritarian values are law and order. In Trump's value system, nonwhites and non-Christians are the chief threats to law and order. Trump knows that reality does not call for a value-system like his; violent crime is at almost historic lows in the United States. Trump is thundering about a crime wave of historic proportions, because he is an authoritarian using his speech to define a simple reality that legitimates his value system, leading voters to adopt it. Its strength is that it conveys his power to define reality. Its weakness is that it obviously contradicts it.

And thus, Trump has public support from the KKK and Nazi groups for a reason; and that support is distinct from public support for any of the other presidential candidates, none of which draw hate groups into the light.

In *A Dialogue* between James Baldwin and Nikki Giovanni, Baldwin argues, "The reason people think it's important to be white is that they think it's important not to be black":

> It's not the world that was my oppressor, because what the world does to you, if the world does it to you long enough and effectively enough, you begin to do to yourself. You become a collaborator, an accomplice of your

own murderers, because you believe the same things they do. They think it's important to be white and you think it's important to be white; they think it's a shame to be black and you think it's a shame to be black. And you have no corroboration around you of any other sense of life.

Yes, we must be vigilant about the white gaze and the male gaze[45], both of which, as Baldwin witnessed, corrupt the agent and object of that gaze, but we must be as vigilant about the white male accusatory finger designed to keep everyone else's gaze somewhere other than where the most power, and too often, the most evil reside.

Dark Mourning in America: "The world is at least/fifty percent terrible"

The best lack all conviction, while the worst
Are full of passionate intensity.
"The Second Coming," William Butler Yeats

Although humans appear ultimately incapable of listening to and then acting upon our great capacity for art—which is an extension of our great capacity for compassion, love, and good—literature may offer some solace in a time when the U.S. has announced itself still a racist, sexist, and xenophobic people, hiding behind the codes of "conservative," "family values," and "Christian nation."

How low do people have to stoop before they have their Lady Macbeth moment?

Out, damned spot! out, I say!--One: two: why,
then, 'tis time to do't.--Hell is murky!--Fie, my

lord, fie! a soldier, and afeard? What need we
fear who knows it, when none can call our power to
account?--Yet who would have thought the old man
to have had so much blood in him.

Shakespeare's dramatization of guilt and *being complicit* is,
let's not ignore, an allusion to Pontius Pilate and the "assassina-
tion" of Jesus[46]:

When Pilate saw that he was getting nowhere, but that
instead an uproar was starting, he took water and washed
his hands in front of the crowd. "I am innocent of this
man's blood," he said. "It is your responsibility!" [Mat-
thew 27:24, NIV]

If we can have that moment in which we admit, confront, and
atone for our responsibility in the evil that humans do, we must
finally listen to James Baldwin:

This rigid refusal to look at ourselves may well destroy us; particularly now since if
we cannot understand ourselves we will not be able to understand anything. - James
Baldwin, "Lockridge: 'The American Myth'"

And to Langston Hughes:

O, let America be America again—
The land that never has been yet—
And yet must be—the land where every man is free.
The land that's mine—the poor man's, Indian's, Negro's,
    ME—
Who made America,
Whose sweat and blood, whose faith and pain,
Whose hand at the foundry, whose plow in the rain,
Must bring back our mighty dream again. ("Let America
    Be America Again")

And face our children with our failures, against which Maggie Smith struggles:

Life is short, though I keep this from my children....
The world is at least
fifty percent terrible, and that's a conservative
estimate, though I keep this from my children....
Life is short and the world
is at least half terrible, and for every kind
stranger, there is one who would break you,
though I keep this from my children. ("Good Bones")

The U.S. and its majority white population have the greatest opportunity before them, a free and powerful nation of riches, and daily, that opportunity is squandered because of our "rigid refusal to look at ourselves."

The U.S. is undeniably inequitable, and to balance among gender, race, etc., we have only two options: to take away or to give to—but in either case, white privilege is erased and white sensibilities are challenged.

There is no evidence the white majority has the ethical backbone to make changes for equity or even to tolerate them.

On a dark mourning in America, I recommend reading or rereading Margaret Atwood's *The Handmaid's Tale*—a sobering imagining of the worst of white responses to the rise of the Others they have created.

We are now on that path, and it is ours to make the decision to turn around or move forward into that oblivion.

The Rights and Responsibilities of the Teacher of English Redux (2016)

"All we gotta do is be brave
And be kind"
"Baby, We'll Be Fine," The National

…the world is gone daft with this nonsense.
John Proctor, *The Crucible*, Arthur Miller

In a keynote address at the 1960 National Council of Teachers of English (NCTE) annual convention, former NCTE president Lou LaBrant asserted:

Every teacher of English exercises some rights, no matter how dictatorial the system under which [she/]he works;

and every teacher carries out some responsibilities. But today we have a considerable movement in this country to curtail certain freedom—rights—of the classroom teacher, and those rights are the matter of this discussion. (p. 379)

Published as "The Rights and Responsibilities of the Teacher of English" in the September 1961 *English Journal*, this characteristic call to action from LaBrant resonated in 2016 as English teachers prepared to gather in Atlanta, Georgia for #NCTE16 with the increasingly important theme of Faces of Advocacy.

Fifty-five years ago, LaBrant advocated for teaching:

Teaching, unlike the making of a car, is primarily a thought process. A [hu]man may work on an assembly line, turning a special kind of bolt day after day, and succeed as a bolt-turner....But the teacher is something quite different from the [hu]man who turns a bolt, because the student is not like a car. Teaching is a matter of changing the mind of the student, of using that magic by which the thinking of one so bears on the thinking of another that new understanding and new mental activity begin. Obviously, the degree to which this is reduced to a mechanical procedure affects the results. (p. 380)

Most practicing teachers today work *within* and *against* political and bureaucratic forces that "[reduce teaching] to a mechanical procedure." And even more disturbing is LaBrant's warning:

What I am trying to say here is that the teacher who is not thinking, testing, experimenting, and exploring the world of thought with which [she/]he deals and the very materials with which [she/]he works, that teacher is a robot [her/]himself. But we cannot expect a teacher to continue the attempt to find better means or to invent new approaches unless [she/]he knows [she/]he will have freedom to use [her/]his results. Without this freedom we must expect either a static teacher or a frustrated one. I have seen both: the dull, hopeless, discouraged teacher, and the angry, blocked, unhappy individual. (p. 380)

At mid-twentieth century, LaBrant spoke against the all-too-familiar "bad" teacher myth[47] used in contemporary calls for accountability:

Repeatedly when capable teachers ask for freedom, some-one points out that we have many lazy teachers, stupid teachers unable to think and choose, ignorant teachers; in short, bad teachers who need control. We do have some, but we encourage others to be bad. Even the weak teacher does better when [she/]he has to face [her/]his own deci-sions, and when [she/]he supports that decision. (p. 383)

The de-professionalizing of all teachers, then, is not something new, but a historical fact of being a teacher. However, LaBrant confronted the culpability among educators themselves:

One reason so many of us do not have our rights is that we have not earned them. The teacher who is free to decide when and how to teach language structure has an obligation to master [her/]his grammar, to analyze the problems of writing, and to study their relations to structure....But [her/]his right to choose comes only when [she/]he has read and considered methods other than [her/]his own. [She/]He has no right to choose

methods or materials which research has proved ineffective....There is little point in asking for a right without
preparation for its use. (p. 390)

"Throughout our country today we have great pressure to
improve our schools," lamented LaBrant. "By far too much of that
pressure tends toward a uniformity, a conformity, a lock-step which
precludes the very excellence we claim to desire":

> There is little consideration of the teacher as a catalyst,
> a changing, growing personality. Only a teacher who
> thinks about [her/]his work can think in class; only a
> thinking teacher can stimulate as they should be stimu-
> lated the minds with which [she/]he works. Freedom of
> any sort is a precious thing; but freedom to be our best,
> in the sense of our highest, is not only our right but our
> moral responsibility. "They"—the public, the administra-
> tors, the critics—have no right to take freedom from us,
> the teachers; but freedom is not something one wins and
> then possesses; freedom is something we rewin every day,
> as much a quality of ourselves as it is a concession from
> others. (pp. 390-391)

The Rights and Responsibilities of the Teacher of English Redux

"Evil settles into everyday life when people are unable or
unwilling to recognize it," writes Teju Cole in the wake of Donald
Trump being elected president of the U.S. "It makes its home
among us when we are keen to minimize it or describe it as something else" ("A Time for Refusal," *The New York Times*).

LaBrant wrote about the field of teaching English throughout the 1940s and 1950s with the power—both for evil and for good—of language forefront of her concerns:

> Misuse of language, as Hitler demonstrated, is a terrible thing; we teachers of English can at the very least teach our students that language is a tool of thought, a tool which can be sharp and keen, but is easily blunted. ("The Individual and His Writing," 1950, p. 265)

So teachers of English/ELA—and all educators—are confronted with a "[m]isuse of language" that has given rise to a presidency built on racism, sexism, and xenophobia; therefore, as during LaBrant's career, we teachers of English/ELA must embrace the most pressing responsibilities.

But driving Trump's and his supporters' bigotry has been a powerful corruption of language: blatant lies, denials of those lies, and the ugliest of coded language. In short, bullying has rewarded a political leader with the highest office in a free society.

Parody of Trump's misuse of language[48] cannot be taken lightly, but that misuse has real consequences on the lives of vulnerable and marginalized people, including children in the classrooms of teachers across the U.S.

Immediately, then, teachers must admit "that every dimension of schooling and every form of educational practice are politically contested spaces" (Joe L. Kincheloe, *Critical Pedagogy Primer*, 2005).

In other words, although teachers are historically and currently de-professionalized by being told not to be political, as LaBrant argued, educators cannot reinforce that mantra by calling for politics-free zones in our classrooms and in our professional spaces.

Calling for no politics is a political act of silencing that brazenly takes a masked political stand in favor of the status quo. Teaching and learning are unavoidably "politically contested spaces," but they are unavoidably *ethically* contested spaces as well.

Language is a human behavior that allows us to wrestle with and find our moral grounding; and thus, those teaching literacy have a profoundly ethical mission to work toward the Right, Good, and Decent—in the act of teaching but also as a personal model. As philosopher Aaron Simmons argues in "Can We Still Do Philosophy?":

> It matters that we demonstrate critical thinking even while others assume that shouting louder is tantamount to evidential refutation. It matters that we think well when it seems hard to think anything at all. It matters that we care about truth because only then can lies and bullshit still be categories to avoid.

The naive stance of neutrality can no longer be who teachers are because, as I noted above, to be neutral is to support the status quo, and in the U.S., the status quo is a cancer that left untreated promises to kill us all.

"It goes without saying, then, that language is also a political instrument, means, and proof of power," James Baldwin wrote in 1979, "If Black English Isn't a Language, Then Tell Me, What Is?"; "It is the most vivid and crucial key to identify: It reveals the private identity, and connects one with, or divorces one from, the larger, public, or communal identity."

Just as LaBrant linked language and power, Baldwin extended that dynamic to include race—and called for using that power in the name of community instead of divisiveness.

The word "critical," now, has taken on exponential layers of meaning.

We are in critical times, and thus, as Kincheloe explains about the political and ethical responsibilities of being critical educator who seeks for students critical literacy:

> Recognition of these educational politics suggests that teachers take a position and make it understandable to their students. *They do not, however, have the right to impose these positions on their students* [emphasis in original]....

> To refuse to name the forces that produce human suffering and exploitation is to take a position that supports oppression and powers that perpetuate it. The argument that any position opposing the actions of dominant power wielders is problematic. It is tantamount to saying that one who admits her oppositional political sentiments and makes them known to students is guilty of indoctrination, while one who hides her consent to dominant power and the status quo it has produced from her students is operating in an objective and neutral manner. Critical pedagogy wants to know who's indoctrinating whom. (p. 11)

In its simple form, to call a lie, a lie; to name racism, racism; to reject hate as hate—these are the undeniable responsibilities of teachers, especially teachers of English/ELA.

To say "I'm neutral" in the face of a lie is to lie.

To say "I'm neutral" in the face of racism is racism, in the face of sexism is sexism, in the face of xenophobia is xenophobia.

To divorce the act of teaching from the world within which it resides is to abdicate the greatest potential of teaching and learning: *to change the human experience from dark to light.*

If we shun our responsibilities as teachers now, we are turning our backs to the ugliest realities faced by Baldwin nearly forty years ago:

> The brutal truth is that the bulk of white people in American never had any interest in educating black people, except as this could serve white purposes. It is not the black child's language that is in question, it is not his language that is despised: It is his experience. A child cannot be taught by anyone who despises him, and a child cannot afford to be fooled. A child cannot be taught by anyone whose demand, essentially, is that the child repudiate his experience, and all that gives him sustenance, and enter a limbo in which he will no longer be black, and in which he knows that he can never become white. Black people have lost too many black children that way.
>
> And, after all, finally, in a country with standards so untrustworthy, a country that makes heroes of so many criminal mediocrities, a country unable to face why so many of the nonwhite are in prison, or on the needle, or standing, futureless, in the streets—it may very well be that both the child, and his elder, have concluded that they have nothing whatever to learn from the people of

a country that has managed to learn so little.

Writing two decades before her NCTE keynote examined above, LaBrant made a foundational request: "For these reasons my first request of every American teacher of English is that [she/] he teach in [her/]his classroom this honest use of language and an understanding of its relation to life" ("English in the American Scene," 1941, p. 206).

And about "this honest use of language," there are only two options—although remaining neutral is not one of them.

The "R" Word as Taboo in Twenty-First Century U.S.A.

Margaret Atwood's *The Handmaid's Tale* offers a not-too-distant dystopia in which Atwood explores the rise of a theocracy as a sanctuary for the declining white race; the work is a tour-de-force confrontation of sexism and misogyny as well as dramatization of the relationship between power and language, including the power inherent in what humans name* and what humans taboo.

The central handmaid of the tale, June/Offred, narrates her own journey through hell that includes being assigned to a Commander who monthly is charged with attempting to impregnate his handmaid in what this new nation of Gilead calls the Ceremony, infusing the act with religious and official overtones.

However, June/Offred characterizes the Ceremony with a disturbing and clinical precision:

> My red skirt is hitched up to my waist, though no higher. Below it the Commander is fucking. What he is fucking

is the lower part of my body. I do not say making love, because this is not what he's doing. Copulating too would be inaccurate, because it would imply two people and only one is involved. Nor does rape cover it: nothing is going on here that I haven't signed up for. There wasn't a lot of choice but there was some, and this is what I chose. (p. 94)

Many aspects of this passage are worth emphasizing, but let's focus on the importance and value in June/Offred naming accurately this awful thing happening—and not ignore the weight of taboo language (such as the word "fucking").

"I have guarded my name as people/ in other times kept their own clipped hair," opens Barbara Kingsolver's poem, "Naming Myself," "believing the soul could be scattered/ if they were careless."

Here too are the intersections of naming, gender, and power: why must women abandon their names in the legal/religious act of marriage while men retain theirs?

Kingsolver's speaker, like Atwood's narrator, both uses and values language as power—guarding a name and naming.

The election of Donald Trump as the president of the U.S. comes in the wake of Trump making inflammatory comments about Mexicans, Muslims, and women. Nonpartisan and measured assessments of Trump's words rightly label them as racist, xenophobic, and sexist/misogynistic.

The rise of Trump as a political leader has exposed the lingering taboo in the U.S. for *naming racism*, even when there is direct evidence of racist language and behavior and especially when that racism is coded (getting tough on crime, building a wall, evoking the specter of terrorism).

Serious public debate has parsed making the distinction between Trump being *a* racist and Trump courting and/or attracting racists, such as being endorsed by the KKK, neo-Nazi organizations, and the white nationalist movement.

A perverse shift has occurred, in fact, from the mislabeling of Barack Obama's being elected president as proof that the U.S. is a post-racial society to Trump's rise asking the U.S. to reconsider what counts as racism.

Trump personifies the triple-Teflon of being white, male, and affluent, most notably in the power of those attributes to deflect the label "racist." As Trump himself asserted defiantly:

> I can never apologize for the truth. I don't mind apologizing for things. But I can't apologize for the truth. I said tremendous crime is coming across. Everybody knows that's true. And it's happening all the time. So, why, when I mention, all of a sudden I'm a racist. I'm not a racist. I don't have a racist bone in my body.[49]

Trump's own strategy frames his words and behavior as "truth," therefore not "racist."

The election of Trump, grounded significantly in white voter support including a majority of white women, adds another layer of tension in that if Trump has voiced racism and/or practiced racism, how complicit are voters as racists themselves? In short, are the approximately 25% of eligible voters who supported Trump racists? And if so, who can name that racism?

A valued colleague who is a rhetorician posted on social media his argument that white liberal elites, especially, should stop naming people as racists—pointing to the overwhelming evidence that the approach is ineffective.[50]

Faced with evidence of racism, whites tend to emphasize their own personal struggles, and many whites now believe racism toward whites trumps racism toward blacks.[51]

Systemic racism (distinct from individual racists) tends to be much harder for many in the U.S. to name or confront. For example, the political and media perpetuation of black-on-black crime is enduring despite the fact that overall crime is mostly intra-racial—the white-on-white crime rate is nearly identical to the black-on-black crime rate.

To approach this in Trump-logic: black-on-black crime rates are true; therefore, referring to them cannot be racist.

But even the racism that can be named in the U.S. is reduced to the most extreme and even cartoonish version that Ta-Nehisi Coates calls the "oafish racist":

Cliven Bundy is old, white, and male. He likes to wave an American flag while spurning the American government and pals around with the militia movement. He does not so much use the word "Negro"—which would be bad enough—but "nigra," in the manner of villain from *Mississippi Burning* or *A Time to Kill*. In short, Cliven Bundy looks, and sounds, much like what white people take racism to be.

The problem with Cliven Bundy isn't that he is a racist but that he is an oafish racist. He invokes the crudest stereotypes, like cotton picking. This makes white people feel bad. ("This Town Needs a Better Class of Racist")

What Trump represents, however, is more insidious:

The elegant racist knows how to injure non-white people while never summoning the specter of white guilt. Elegant racism requires plausible deniability, as when Reagan just happened to stumble into the Neshoba County fair and mention state's rights. Oafish racism leaves no escape hatch, as when Trent Lott praised Strom Thurmond's singularly segregationist candidacy.

Elegant racism is invisible, supple, and enduring. It disguises itself in the national vocabulary, avoids epithets and didacticism. Grace is the singular marker of elegant racism. One should never underestimate the touch needed to, say, injure the voting rights of black people without ever saying their names. Elegant racism lives at the border of white shame. Elegant racism was the poll tax. Elegant racism is voter-ID laws.

The racism of Trump and emboldened by Trump sullies the "elegant," but it certainly meets Coates's recognition of "plausible deniability."

Finally, let's return to June/Offred, being *fucked*, but not *raped* because "[t]here wasn't a lot of choice but there was some." In a free society, black and brown people find themselves in a parallel circumstance to June/Offred, the victims of racism even though "[t]here wasn't a lot of choice but there was some."

And as my colleague noted, victims of racism certainly find value in naming racism and racists.

The problem my colleague raises, however, is among white allies to those victims of racism; if it is ineffective for white allies to name racism, to name racists, what is our obligation as allies against racism and inequity?

To suggest that racism and racists do not exist until acknowledged by whites is a nasty dose of paternalistic racism. To tip-toe around racists for fear of offending them and entrenching racism further also seems like a slap in the face of black and brown people living the very real consequences of racism and the "rigid refusal to look at ourselves" (James Baldwin, "Lockridge: 'The American Myth'").

As a very privileged ally to everyone marginalized by racism (as well as sexism/misogyny, xenophobia, and all sorts of bigotry), I believe I must listen to black and brown voices, but I also must use my privilege to amplify (not confirm) those voices—to stand beside and behind, but never to speak for.

There was a time in the not-so-distant past when even the oafish racist was not called to account; therefore, I am convinced that a key step to erasing elegant racism, systemic racism, is to have the courage to call racists "racists" regardless of the evidence that those rightly labeled "racists" will not change.

I am taking this stand because I am not sure our goal is to change individual *racists*, but to change the greater capacity of the larger population who have yet to confront their culpability in elegant/systemic racism, and thus to create a critical mass in the name of equity that will eradicate racism over time.

In the most profound and bitter sort of appropriateness, the U.S. has elected the very worst and most perfect leader of, as Trump would say, the truth about the U.S.—which is that we are a racist, sexist/misogynist, and xenophobic people, drunk on consumerism and negligent in our humanity for each other.

With that before us and *named,* let us hope we can confess our sins, do our penance, and create a more perfect union.

* Dare we call fascism "fascism"? "No, this isn't the 1930s – but yes, this is fascism," James McDougall

The Zombie Politics of School Choice: A Reader

The original zombie narrative[52] has been re-created and distorted in contemporary U.S. pop culture, as Victoria Anderson explains:

> So what were zombies, originally? The answer lies in the Caribbean. They weren't endlessly-reproducing, flesh-eating ghouls. Instead, the zombie was the somewhat tragic figure of a human being maintained in a catatonic state – a soulless body – and forced to labour for whoever cast the spell over him or her. In other words, the zombie is – or was – a slave. I always find it troubling that, somewhere along the line, we forgot or refused to acknowledge this and have replaced the suffering slave with the figure of a mindless carnivore – one that reproduces, virus-like, with a bite. ("Pride, prejudice and the mutation of zombies from Caribbean slaves to flesh-eaters")

While there is some nuance and variety among the many ways in which U.S. pop culture has manipulated the zombie narrative, central to almost all of those is the zombie as relentless consumer who has risen from the dead and resists being killed permanently.

In that context, school choice is *zombie politics* because the ideology will not die and its many versions (vouchers, tuition tax credits, charter schools) are destructive.

A few decades ago, school choice advocacy depended on the appeal of the ideology itself since choice is idealized and fetishized in the U.S.

Once school choice policy began to be implemented, and then over the past 2-3 decades as evidence from how choice has not achieved the promises made, school choice advocacy has depended on constantly shifting the *type* of choice and the *promises*.

At the center of the school choice debate is a failure in the U.S. to appreciate the importance of the Commons, how publicly funded institutions are necessary for the free market to work (both economically and ethically).

For example, publicly funded roads and highways are powerful and essential for commerce in the U.S. Many resist toll roads in the U.S., and certainly, the entire economy and way of life in the U.S. would be destroyed if we left roads and highways to the whims of the Invisible Hand.

Two facts remain important now as the election of Donald Trump and the apparent choice for Secretary of Education suggest that the zombie politics of school choice has been rejuvenated:

- The overwhelming evidence for all aspects of school choice show little differences when compared to traditional public schools; some aspects can certainly be categorized as harmful, and any so-called positives are erased when those gains are explained—attrition, comparing apples and oranges, selectivity, inability to scale, etc.

- Idealizing parental choice fails to step back to the bedrock promise of publicly funded institutions: insuring that choice isn't necessary.

Just as a blow to the head and brain can kill permanently the zombie, evidence and truth should eradicate the zombie politics of school choice. However, Trumplandia is a post-truth country.

None the less, the truth is our only real option, so below is a reader to combat the zombie politics of school choice:

"Idealizing, Misreading Impoverished and Minority Parental Choice" [blog]

"Parental Choice, Magical Thinking, and the Paralysis of Indirect Solutions" [blog]

"School choice lessons for Charleston – Post and Courier" [blog]

"Public School, Charter Choice: More Segregation by Design" [blog]

"Don't Buy School Choice Week" [blog]

Parental Choice?: A Critical Reconsideration of Choice and the Debate about Choice, P.L. Thomas

The Public School Advantage: Why Public Schools Outperform Private Schools, Christopher A. Lubienski and Sarah Theule Lubienski

"Research-Based Options for Education Policymaking – 2016 Collection", William J. Mathis (NEPC)

"School Finance 101", Bruce Baker [blog site]

"School Vouchers Are Not a Cure For Segregation: Parts I-V", Jersey Jazzman

"On negative effects of vouchers", Mark Dynarski:

> Recent research on statewide voucher programs in Louisiana and Indiana has found that public school students that received vouchers to attend private schools subsequently scored lower on reading and math tests compared to similar students that remained in public schools. The magnitudes of the negative impacts were large. These studies used rigorous research designs that allow for strong causal conclusions. And they showed that the results were not explained by the particular tests that were used or the possibility that students receiving vouchers transferred out of above-average public schools.
>
> Another explanation is that our historical understanding of the superior performance of private schools is no longer accurate. Since the nineties, public schools have been under heavy pressure to improve test scores. Private schools were exempt from these accountability requirements. A recent study showed that public schools closed the score gap with private schools. That study did not look specifically at Louisiana and Indiana, but trends in scores on the National Assessment of Educational Progress for public school students in those states are similar to national trends.
>
> In education as in medicine, 'first, do no harm' is a powerful guiding principle. A case to use taxpayer funds to

send children of low-income parents to private schools is based on an expectation that the outcome will be positive. These recent findings point in the other direction. More needs to be known about long-term outcomes from these recently implemented voucher programs to make the case that they are a good investment of public funds. As well, we need to know if private schools would up their game in a scenario in which their performance with voucher students is reported publicly and subject to both regulatory and market accountability.

"Failing the Test: A New Series Examines Charter Schools", Bill Raden (*Capital and Main*)

Regardless of motives, the charter initiatives in Oakland and Los Angeles together signal a significant watershed in the growth of a statewide movement that was birthed by California's Charter Schools Act of 1992 to create classroom laboratories that might develop the dynamic new curricula and teaching methods needed to reinvigorate schools that were failing the state's most underserved and disadvantaged children.

How that modest experiment in fixing neighborhood public schools could morph in less than 25 years into the replacement of public schools with an unproven parallel system of privately run, taxpayer-funded academies is only half the story of California's education wars that will be examined in this series, much of which is based on conversations with both sides of the charter school debate. Over the next few days Capital & Main will also look at:

- The influence wielded by libertarian philanthropists who bankroll the 50-50 takeovers.

- How charter schools spend less time and money on students with learning disabilities.

- The lack of charter school transparency and accountability.

- How charter expansion is pushing Oakland's public school district toward a fateful tipping point.

- The success of less radical yet more effective reforms that get scant media coverage.

- Nine solution takeaways for struggling schools.

"Charters and Access: Here is Evidence", Julian Vasquez Helig

"No, Eva, You Can't Do Whatever You Want", Jersey Jazzman

"Don't Trust Invested Advocates in Edureform Wars" [blog], P.L. Thomas

The struggle for control of public education: Market ideology vs. democratic values. Michael Engel (2001), Temple University Press:

> [I]t is nothing short of disastrous that more than ever before, one antidemocratic system of ideas—market ideology—almost exclusively defines the terms of educational politics and charts the path of education reform

> …[I]deology is important in understanding educational change….Ideology is nonetheless often overlooked or at best misapplied by mainstream social scientists as a factor in politics. This is due in part to the dominance of quantitative methodologies in political science, which

leads to the trivialization of the concept into conveniently measurable but irrelevant labels....Market ideology has triumphed over democratic values not because of its superiority as a theory of society but in part because in a capitalist system it has an inherent advantage. (pp. 3, 8-9)

Education and the cult of efficiency: A study of the social forces that have shaped the administration of the public schools. Raymond E. Callahan (1962), The University of Chicago Press:

> For while schools everywhere reflect to some extent the culture of which they are a part and respond to forces within that culture, the American public schools, because of the nature of their pattern of organization, support, and control, were especially vulnerable and responded quickly to the strongest social forces. . . .The business influence was exerted upon education in several ways: through newspapers, journals, and books; through speeches at educational meetings; and, more directly, through actions of school boards. It was exerted by laymen, by professional journalists, by businessmen or industrialists either individually or in groups. . ., and finally by educators themselves. Whatever its source, the influence was exerted in the form of suggestions or demands that the schools be organized and operated in a more businesslike way and that more emphasis by placed upon a practical and immediately useful education....
>
> The tragedy itself was fourfold: that educational questions were subordinated to business considerations; that administrators were produced who were not, in any true sense, educators; that a scientific label was put on some

very unscientific and dubious methods and practices; and that an anti-intellectual climate, already prevalent, was strengthened. (pp. 1, 5-6, 246)

Trumplandia 2016 (Prelude): What Mainstream Media Hath Wrought

The election of Barack Obama prompted a rash claim that the U.S. was officially post-racial. As a cruel commentary on that misinterpretation of the first black president, the era of Donald Trump has coincided with the Oxford Dictionary naming "post-truth" the word of the year.

Part of being "post-truth" includes that which shall not be named.

For example, "[a]n Alabama police officer has been fired for sharing racist memes, including one about Michelle Obama," reports Lindsey Bever in "Alabama officer fired over racist meme calling Michelle Obama 'fluent in ghetto'" for *The Washington Post*. But the police department's explanation for the firing is important to analyze:

Bryant, the city manager, said statements that are "deemed to be biased or racially insensitive or derogatory" can affect the community's trust in the police department and, when that happens, "we have to take action to correct it."

Not racist, not racism, but "racially insensitive." While Bever does use "racist" in the lede, later she explains:

Since Donald Trump was elected president, a wave of racially and religiously motivated acts of intimidation, violence and harassment have swept across the country — from a middle school in Michigan and a high school in Pennsylvanian to universities in Texas and elsewhere.

Not a wave of racism, but "racially motivated acts."

And while this article and the incidences Bever details are mostly about how racists and racism have been confronted and with consequences (multiple firings of public officials), the piece still reflects the tendency in the U.S. for mainstream media to avoid or tiptoe around directly naming racists and racism.

Tressie McMillan Cottom, an assistant professor of sociology at Virginia Commonwealth University and faculty associate with Harvard University's Berkman Klein Center for Internet & Society, explains in a detailed blog post:

I said over two years ago that media style guides precluded major newspapers from calling something racist.

Then I asked around and professional media people told me that there isn't a style convention on this matter so much as an informal culture. The general rule, I was told, is to never call anything racist and certainly to never call anyone racist. At best, they might quote someone calling something or someone racist.

The implication is that there is no such thing as objectively racist. Racism, according to many mainstream media producers and gatekeepers, can only be subjective. ("Racism With No Racists: The President Trump Conundrum")

While, again, Bever's journalism is relatively bold in this context identified by Cottom, the authority figure in the article represents well a fundamental problem in the U.S. with naming racists and racism.

For example, in 2014, when high school students dressed in black face for intramural football, the principal reacted as follows:

A group of seniors in Sullivan, Missouri was criticized after donning blackface for an intramural football the *Riverfront Times* reported.

"I thought, 'Oh, they don't mean anything by it. Just let it go. No one thinks anything of it,'" Sullivan High School principal Jennifer Schmidt. "I didn't think anyone did. Evidently, someone did."

Schmidt said the 12 seniors painted their faces black on Nov. 5 as part of a charity "powder-puff" football game organized by the junior class. According to her, the face paint was intended to be a parody of the football team's habit of wearing eye-black on their own faces. ("Missouri HS principal on seniors' blackface stunt: 'They don't mean anything by it,'" Arturo Garcia 19 November

2014, *Raw Story*)

Broadly, then, although in the U.S. there is lip service given to the importance of a free press in a democracy, the real problem is that there is no critical free press—one instead that honors a careless "both sides" and "press release" journalism over offering the public informed stances.

In the prelude to the era of Trumplandia, we were faced with how the lack of a critical free press either *allowed* or *created* Trump and how the rise of a critical free press could suppress the danger inherent in Trump's tenure as president and turn the tide against bigotry.

A vivid example of the dangers of the traditionally passive mainstream media is the coverage of Trump considering former DC chancellor Michelle Rhee for Secretary of Education; for example, Andrew Ujifusa in *Education Week*:

> Trump's search for education secretary appears to be crossing party lines. Rhee, who has identified as a Democrat throughout her career, is a strong supporter of school choice (including vouchers), which appears to be the top K-12 priority for Trump. She also rose to prominence for how she handled teachers and teacher evaluations during her tenure in the District of Columbia, which lasted from 2007 to 2010. In 2010, she left the nation's capital and founded StudentsFirst, an advocacy group that pushes for choice, reforms to labor policies often unfriendly to teachers' unions, and data-based school accountability. She stepped down as the leader of StudentsFirst in 2014. ("Trump to Meet Michelle Rhee as Education Secretary Search Continues")

Framed as crossing party lines, and then detailing in Wikipedia fashion Rhee's professional resume, this coverage ignores Rhee's lack of experience in education (a Teach For America corp member) as well as her tenure in DC that was either significantly mismanaged or outright criminal—omitting as well that Rhee's husband, Kevin Johnson, is also a seriously tarnished public official.

Even more telling is Ujifusa's use of the standard mainstream journalism "both sides" reduction of all issues—some will applaud Rhee and some will not. Of course, no effort is made to make an informed recognition that Rhee is, like Trump, so tarnished in her career that she is unsuited for public service.

Those in positions of authority and the mainstream media who report on them are both trapped in maintaining and creating a safe space throughout the U.S. to protect racism, white privilege, and sexism/misogyny from being named. As Cottom includes about this phenomenon:

> The most cited and widely recognized [research] is Eduardo Bonilla-Silva's theory of colorblind racism in which there is racism but no racists....

> Media had, at some point, produced a culture that normalized using euphemisms for racism and racists.

And so, in Trumplandia, not only is truth sacrificed, but also is any semblance of expertise, credibility, or ethics.

The consequence of that approach is Trump himself and now the government he has the power to build.

The only antidote to perpetuating bigotry is to name it—

including especially by a critical free press that could be a powerful force for a free people.

Daring to Confront Race and Class through Poetry in Trumplandia

My mind is racing, as it always will
My hands tired, my heart aches
"Half a World Away," R.E.M.

Writing specifically about Mark Twain's *Adventures of Huckleberry Finn* and drawing on powerful words from Toni Morrison, Jocelyn Chadwick, writing as president-elect of the National Council of Teachers of English (NCTE), argues in "We Dare Not Teach What We Know We Must: The Importance of Difficult Conversations":

Our ELA classrooms take our children around the world and beyond—into past, present, and future worlds. We provide safe and trusted spaces for them where difficult conversations can and do take place. If at times teachers, at whatever level they teach, hit a roadblock, perhaps this impediment is due to or own predilections of codifying our students, stereotyping them before we even listen to them, much less get to know them....[T]he last time I checked, we teach students—not colors, not types. Perhaps it is we who need to stop and reread all of the texts we teach from the 21st-century perspective of students' empowerment—empowerment that our literature provides....It has been some of us who have been demurring, listening to the voices of others, telling us we dare not teach what we know we must. (p. 91)

Published in *English Journal* in the month the U.S. elected Donald Trump, Chadwick's confrontation of "some of us who have been demurring" and "difficult conversations" resonates in ways, I suspect, that even Chadwick may not have anticipated.

Toni Morrison's words after the election also serve teachers of English Language Arts in the same way that Chadwick anchors her argument about our classrooms, the literature we explore, and the discussions we encourage and allow:

On Election Day, how eagerly so many white voters— both the poorly educated and the well educated— embraced the shame and fear sowed by Donald Trump. The candidate whose company has been sued by the Justice Department for not renting apartments to black people. The candidate who questioned whether Barack Obama was born in the United States, and who seemed to condone the beating of a Black Lives Matter protester at a campaign rally. The candidate who kept black workers off the floors of his casinos. The candidate who is

beloved by David Duke and endorsed by the Ku Klux
Klan. ("Mourning for Whiteness")

In Morrison's lament, we must recognize the weight of both
race and social class on the American character. Morrison confronts white privilege and the consequences of that privilege being
eroded: "These people are not so much angry as terrified, with the
kind of terror that makes knees tremble."

As teachers of ELA, it is ours to dare, to dare to teach openly
against the world within which our students live and within which
our classrooms exist. In the spirit of Chadwick's call to re-read,
and I would add re-teach, literature in that light, please consider
how Barbara Kingsolver's "What the Janitor Heard in the Elevator"
from her collection *Another America/Otra America* provides "safe
and trusted spaces" for investigating the increased problems with
race and social class in Trumplandia America.

Barbara Kingsolver's "What the Janitor Heard in the Elevator"

Kingsolver is best recognized as a novelist—notably for her
The Poisonwood Bible—but she is also a brilliant essayist, a skillful
poet, and an activist who lives her activism.

Her sole collection of poetry, *Another America/Otra America*,
reflects the essential political nature characterizing all of Kingsolver's work and is published as a bi-lingual collection of Spanish and English versions of all poems (Rebeca Cartes translates
Kingsolver's original English into Spanish).

"What the Janitor Heard in the Elevator" provides traditional opportunities to highlight the craft of writing and of poetry, including (through which I will discuss the poem more directly later):

- The importance and power of titles.

- Word choice, connotation, and framing/motifs.

- Pronouns and ambiguity.

- Character and plot in genres/modes beyond fictional narratives.

To frame the poem in the context of the world within which our students live, however, means that students should be allowed and even invited to connect Kingsolver's craft with the tensions in public discourse about race and class after the election of Donald Trump—concerns about "deplorables" and debates about if and how to understand white anger/fear as well as the increased focus on the white working class. The poem reads in full:

The woman in the gold bracelets tells her friend:
I had to fire another one.
Can you believe it?
She broke the vase
Jack gave me for Christmas.
It was one of those,
you know? That worked
with everything. All my colors.
I asked him if he'd mind
if I bought one again just like it.
It was the only one that just always worked.

Her friend says:
Find another one that speaks English.

That's a plus.

The woman in the gold agrees
that is a plus.

A first reading of the poem should include asking students about the janitor in the title—Who do they see? Is that janitor they envision black or brown? What do they notice about the presence of the janitor in the poem itself?

Here, the students can see how racialized their perceptions are, and then discuss the tension between the janitor being in the elevator and the title, but *invisible* in the lines of the poem as well as to the two women.

How does the poem create a space to discuss the marginalization of people by race, by profession, and by social class?

This central question is further complicated in the poem's use of color imagery, diction, and pronouns.

In the first line "gold bracelets" triggers social class that shades the conversation between friends (again, who do students see when they imagine these women?) that is being *overheard* by the janitor in the elevator. Voiceless and seemingly invisible to these women with at least relative affluence, the janitor may represent those same conditions in the U.S. for people of color and people from the working class.

The comments by the "woman in the gold bracelets" are layered and coded:

- She refers to her fired domestic help as "one" and then also refers to the broken vase as "one"—the ambiguity of the pronoun usage reducing the worker to an object.

- Word choices such as "worked" and "colors" connote "worker" and "colored" if we extend the poem to race and social class.

- The suggestion in her comments ("another one") triggers the implication that the worker is expendable, replaceable, just as the vase *may* be, although the women appears more concerned with replacing the vase.

And then, the friend's response forces the reader to reconsider or re-examine a first read with "one that speaks English"—more directly invoking the race and nationality of the worker and opening a door to the political and public debates about undocumented workers.

Presented with a bi-lingual collection, how many students initially see a black man as janitor, but then after the friend's comment, rethink that assumption since the poem appears to be interrogating the tensions of race, class, and language between whites and Latinx?

The final two lines bring the reader back to "gold," which frames the poem in color imagery that speaks to materialism and affluence as well as opulence.

Chadwick quotes Morrison on teaching: "Open doors, let them in, give permission, and see what happens. Students make you think. I learn faster and more when I am teaching."

And while I am skeptical of universality, I am enamored by the *enduring* that is art, that is literature. Kingsolver's poem opens doors for her readers—to the enduring tensions of race, social class, and language; to the specter of invisibility and what Arundhati Roy has explained in her "The 2004 Sydney Peace Prize lecture" as: "We know of course there's really no such thing as the 'voiceless.' There are only the deliberately silenced, or the preferably unheard"; and to debates about naming racism and racists.

All texts, *all* poetry, and then *this* poem—as Chadwick acknowledges, "we teach students" who live in a flawed and complex world not of their making.

Teachers of ELA have unique responsibilities to engage with our students and the world through the texts we choose and the texts students choose as open doors into the world that our students could build instead.

Barbara Kingsolver: "everything we do becomes political: speaking up or not speaking up"

"So many of us have stood up for the marginalized," explains writer Barbara Kingsolver in the wake of Trumplandia, "but never expected to be here ourselves," adding:

> It happened to us overnight, not for anything we did wrong but for what we know is right. Our first task is to stop shaming ourselves and claim our agenda. It may feel rude, unprofessional and risky to break the habit of respecting our government; we never wanted to be enemies of the state. But when that animosity mounts against us, everything we do becomes political: speaking up or not speaking up. Either one will have difficult consequences. That's the choice we get. ("Trump changed everything. Now everything counts")

She then calls for those of us with a social justice conscience to wear our hearts on our sleeves, including teachers:

> If we're teachers we explicitly help children of all kinds feel safe in our classrooms under a bullying season that's already opened in my town and probably yours. Language used by a president may enter this conversation. We say wrong is wrong.

I have been using the writing of Kingsolver in both my high school English classes and a variety of college courses since the 1990s, and my first book-length examination of teaching a writer focused on Kingsolver.

The most enduring writing from Kingsolver for me as a teacher has been her essay writing. And while Kingsolver's politics drives her fiction—such as *Flight Behavior*—and her poetry, there is a artistry to her essays that allows her politics to meander instead of immediately provoking.

For example, her collection *Small Wonder* grew out of 9/11, and the essays speak powerfully with a progressive voice that is unlike the American character and that challenges the flag-waving patriotism/nationalism the terrorism spurred across the U.S.

And while Kingsolver actually lives her convictions, her newest confrontation of what Trump means for the U.S. reads as an intensified Kingsolver-as-activist.

"We refuse to disappear," she announces.

The American character has long misread and misrepresented the label "political," and the rise of Trump may have, as Kingsolver argues, brought about inadvertently the change promised by

Obama: "everything we do becomes political: speaking up or not speaking up. Either one will have difficult consequences."

But only one—speaking up in the name of the good and the equitable—has the potential for the sort of consequences a free people should be seeking.

I, Too, Am a Dangerous Professor if You Covet Ignorance, Hatred

We Marxists are rightfully criticized for being idealistic, but we are unfairly demonized by those across the U.S. who wrongly associate Marxism, socialism, and communism with totalitarian governments and human oppression.

You see, Marxism as a scholarly stance is a *moral* stance—unlike the amoral pose of capitalism.

We Marxist academics and scholars are all about the good, the right, and the equitable—including creating intellectually challenging classrooms in which every student feels physically and psychologically safe.

But this is Trumplandia, a sort of Bizarro World in which reality TV has become a real-life nightmare, including a professor watch list promoted by an Orwellian right-wing organization that claims to be protecting free speech and academic freedom by identifying dangerous professors.

George Yancy, professor of philosophy at Emory University, has responded with the powerful "I Am a Dangerous Professor," and my home state of South Carolina has had three professors included on the list.

The responses to the list have run a range from fear (because professors have received very serious threats) to bemusement to anger about *not* being included.

I am a white male full professor with tenure, but I teach in the South—where before I joined a university faculty, I was an intellectually closeted public school teacher for 18 stressful years.

As a leftist and atheist, I was constantly vigilant to mask who I was, what I believe and live, because I was fearful of losing my job and career (SC is an Orwellian-named "right to work" state) *that I dearly love.*

When I interviewed for my current position, I was about as naive and idealistic as a person could be about the golden fields of higher education.

During my model lesson for my day-long interview, I explained to the class I was a critical pedagogue, and thus offering a Marxist perspective on literacy and power.

Later in the day, at the debriefing and in hushed tones, I was told I may want to *not* share the whole Marxist thing if hired at the university.

I was hired—although my being a critical educator, scholar, and public intellectual have all been problematic throughout my second career as a professor.

And I have bull-headedly remained true to my ethics as both

a professor/teacher and a critical pedagogue, best expressed by my
dear friend and mentor Joe Kincheloe:

> Thus, proponents of critical pedagogy understand that
> every dimension of schooling and every form of educa-
> tional practice are politically contested spaces. Shaped
> by history and challenged by a wide range of interest
> groups, educational practice is a fuzzy concept as it takes
> place in numerous settings, is shaped by a plethora of
> often-invisible forces, and can operate even in the name
> of democracy and justice to be totalitarian and oppres-
> sive. (p. 2)

> Recognition of these educational politics suggests that
> teachers take a position and make it understandable
> to their students. *They do not, however, have the right
> to impose these positions on their students* [emphasis in
> original]....

> In this context it is not the advocates of critical peda-
> gogy who are most often guilty of impositional teaching
> but many of the mainstream critics themselves. When
> mainstream opponents of critical pedagogy promote
> the notion that all language and political behavior that
> oppose the dominant ideology are forms of indoctrina-
> tion, they forget how experience is shaped by unequal
> forms of power. To refuse to name the forces that produce
> human suffering and exploitation is to take a position
> that supports oppression and powers that perpetuate it.
> The argument that any position opposing the actions of
> dominant power wielders is problematic. It is tantamount
> to saying that one who admits her oppositional political

sentiments and makes them known to students is guilty of indoctrination, while one who hides her consent to dominant power and the status quo it has produced from her students is operating in an objective and neutral manner. Critical pedagogy wants to know who's indoctrinating whom. (*Critical Pedagogy Primer*, p. 11)

In fact, during the fall of 2016 in my foundations of education course, I reiterated to the class that as a Marxist I often seem obnoxious, even dogmatic because I teach and speak with a moral imperative, an impassioned moral imperative—seeking that which is right, good, and equitable.

About this watch list, then, I am torn, struggling between embracing Yancy's brilliant rebuttal and my own belief that I am in fact not the dangerous one because the dangerous thing about this world is to remain both ignorant and without a moral grounding.

As a Marxist educator and scholar/public intellectual, as a critical pedagogue, I am not the person hiding who I am or what I am seeking.

The dishonest are those who claim to be objective when in fact they are endorsing uncritically an inequitable status quo.

The dishonest are those claiming a non-political pose that is itself a political pose.

The dishonest are waving flags and chanting the entirely dishonest "Make America Great Again."

That is dangerous stuff—endangering the faint promise of life, liberty, and the pursuit of happiness that I, in fact, hold sacred.

So I am left with this paradox: I, too, am a dangerous professor if you covet ignorance, hatred.

If you are seeking the Truth, however, as well as the right, the good, and the equitable, please call me comrade because I am no danger to you at all.

Adichie's "danger of a single story" and the Rise of Post-Truth Trumplandia

In an effort to understand post-truth Trumplandia, this is one explanation:

Patrick Thornton @pwthornton

Why coverage is so off: Journalists literally have no framework or training with how to deal with a president who denies basic reality.

However, this fails to confront that the rise of Trumplandia is but an extreme and logical extension of a mainstream media and political elite existing almost entirely on false narratives—the denial of basic reality.

The bootstrap and rising boat narratives, black-on-black crime, the pervasive threat of terrorism, the lazy poor, the welfare queen, and the relentless "kids today" mantra—these are all powerful as well as enduring claims but also provably false.

With Trump's election, the post-truth reality now focuses on lamenting the plight of the white working class (also provably false) and masking racism and white supremacy as "alt-right."

The media simply report that Source X makes Claim A—but never venture into the harder story that Source X is *making a false Claim A*—especially when false Claim A rings true within the Great American Myths that Chimamanda Ngozi Adichie powerfully warns about in a 2009 TED Talk, "The Dangers of a Single Story":

> I'm a storyteller. And I would like to tell you a few personal stories about what I like to call "the danger of the single story."…
>
> I come from a conventional, middle-class Nigerian family. My father was a professor. My mother was an administrator. And so we had, as was the norm, live-in domestic help, who would often come from nearby rural villages. So, the year I turned eight, we got a new house boy. His name was Fide. The only thing my mother told us about him was that his family was very poor. My mother sent yams and rice, and our old clothes, to his family. And when I didn't finish my dinner, my mother would say, "Finish your food! Don't you know? People like Fide's family have nothing." So I felt enormous pity for Fide's family.
>
> Then one Saturday, we went to his village to visit, and his mother showed us a beautifully patterned basket made of dyed raffia that his brother had made. I was startled. It had not occurred to me that anybody in his family could actually make something. All I had heard about them was

how poor they were, so that it had become impossible for me to see them as anything else but poor. Their poverty was my single story of them.

Adichie artfully shares more examples in her talk, but her message from 2009 rings much more horrifying today in post-truth Trumplandia, where the elected leader of the free world can say damn near anything one minute, deny it the next, and remain safely cloaked in the lies that endure as the "one story" many in the U.S. believe despite ample evidence to the contrary.

The one story of black men as criminals that allows police to disproportionately execute those black men in the streets.

The one story of the lazy poor that allows political leaders to avoid their moral obligations to provide social services, including health care even for children.

The one story of objectified women that allows rape culture and the democratically elected leader of the free world to boast about his own cavalier behavior as a sexual predator.

And so: "Stories matter. Many stories matter," Adichie concludes:

Stories have been used to dispossess and to malign, but stories can also be used to empower and to humanize. Stories can break the dignity of a people, but stories can also repair that broken dignity.

Post-truth Trumplandia is creeping toward yet another of the very ugliest stories of a people claiming to embrace life and liberty but denying basic reality instead.

The question before us is whether or not we have the capacity for changing that arc of history toward, as Adichie expresses, the possibility to "regain a kind of paradise."

Resisting Fatalism in Post-Truth Trumplandia: Charter Schools and the End of Accountability

Bill asks Mike Campbell how Mike goes bankrupt, and Mike answers: "'Two ways.... Gradually and then suddenly.'"

This conversation in Ernest Hemingway's sparse dramatization of the Lost Generation, *The Sun Also Rises*, also serves as a chilling characterization of how the U.S. finds itself in post-truth Trumplandia.

The paradoxes multiply for those of us in education because we can not only see but also live the reality that our post-truth U.S. is both a consequence of a country's negligence of universal public education and the cause of that negligence—notably the uber-corrosive accountability era of the past three decades.

It seems like a distant memory, but before the rise of Trumplandia, there appeared to be light at the end of the tunnel, a crumbling of support for charter schools on the heels of rising resistance to standards and high-stakes testing.

And then the election of Donald Trump.

And then Trump's apparent selection of a Secretary of Education with zero experience in public education and a harsh school choice agenda.

This feels not like passing dark clouds, but a potential permanent eclipse of the sun.

However, we must resist the alluring fatalism of Trumplandia upon us even though truth and evidence have been declared defunct.

In a time of post-truth, truth becomes Kryptonite.

The Crack in Charter School Support Must Be a Harbinger of the End of the Accountability Era

"What exactly is the position of charter school supporters?" ask educators and activists Adrienne Dixson and Andre Perry, writing "Charter Backers Can Stop the NAACP Moratorium by Meeting These Four Demands" at *The Hechinger Report*. For some, the time to question charter school advocates and commitments to charter schools is well past due because the evidence is substantial[53] that charter advocacy fails against miraculous claims and erodes community public schools.

Nearly three decades ago, charter schools began as educational experiments designed to benefit, not compete with, all public schools, but during the Obama administration, charter schools have increasingly turned into an *alternative* to traditional public schools, especially for black and brown students.

As a softer but misleading and more publicly palpable form of school choice, charter schools represent a microcosm of the larger accountability era of education reform. In many ways, charter schools have been defined by embracing Teach For America (TFA) and rejecting tenure and unionized staffs, focusing on standards and high-stakes testing, promising to close achievement gaps among vulnerable populations of students (black, brown, and poor), and identifying strongly with "no excuses" ideologies and policies such as teaching "grit" and growth mindset, as well as enforcing zero tolerance disciplinary agendas.

The transition from educational experimentation to educational alternative can likely be traced back to 2009, when David Brooks proclaimed the Harlem Children's Zone (HCZ) "The Harlem Miracle" and introduced Paul Tough and Geoffrey Canada to the education reform landscape.

Tough established himself as a powerful proponent of "grit," and "miracle" charter schools, while Canada was soon crowned "Superman" in a controversial and biased documentary that promoted TFA and charters while demonizing unionized teachers.

Grounded in both Barack and Michelle Obama's championing Canada's HCZ, the education agenda of the last eight years has never really questioned charter schools or their advocates. However, at the end of Obama's second term and despite this administration's doubling down on George W. Bush-style accountability education reform, questions about charter school began in some notable places, including by Secretary of Education Arne Duncan penning "The Myth of the 'Miracle School.'"

Ironically, charter schools have now returned to delivering on their original goal: they're an experiment that has quite possibly produced what education reformers could not have anticipated—evidence that the accountability era has failed. Questioning charter schools prompts, then, another question: Can calls for a moratorium on expanding charter schools sustain a broader end to accountability era education reform under Trump?

From "Miracle" to Mirage

Over Obama's two terms, charter schools went from "miracle" status to the focus of a searing satire by HBO's John Oliver, prompting, as Valerie Strauss reports in "John Oliver, they're after you! Charter school backers sponsor $100,000 anti-Oliver video contest" at *The Answer Sheet*: "the Washington-based Center for Education Reform, a nonprofit pro-charter organization, [to offer] $100,000 to the school that creates the best rebuttal video to Oliver's rant."

But the challenges and rebuttals to charter schools have also been extremely serious. Both the NAACP and the Black Lives Matter movement issued calls for a moratorium and an end to charter schools serving highly segregated impoverished and black/ brown students.

The shift from "miracle" to mirage grew out of the utopian promises linked to charter schools, such as closing the achievement gap, paired with the crisis discourse (failing schools and "bad" teachers) around traditional public schools.

Advocates for charter schools blamed low academic outcomes for impoverished and minority students on "bad" teachers and the "soft bigotry of low expectations,"[54] but claimed that charter schools would close the achievement gap, primarily by implementing the major elements of the accountability education reform movement.

The promises of charter schools gradually began to be central to major reform efforts across the U.S.

Notably, one of the most powerful examples of eradicating traditional public schools and replacing them with charter schools—as well as firing the entire teacher workforce and replacing them with mostly TFA recruits—has been New Orleans post-Katrina, documented by education journalist Sarah Carr's *Hope Against Hope*. Yet, since New Orleans became an all-charter school district, test scores have remained low and schools have continued to be plagued by segregation—*the exact problems charters were supposed to eradicate.*

Parental choice, which lies at the heart of support for charters, has failed, as Julian Vasquez Heilig, professor of Educational Leadership and Policy Studies at California State University, has detailed. Broadly, Helig explains:

> Despite the trendy popularity of charter schools in some circles, their wholesale replacement of traditional public schools is unnecessary. Not only do decades of data and research show this, but in each city there are plenty of successful public schools on the other side of the tracks or highway or river. The wealthy in the United States, regardless of locality, continue to have access to quality public education. ("Charters and Access: Here is Evidence")

As an experiment, then, "decades of data" have produced results that charter proponents would like to ignore: on balance, charter schools are mostly indistinguishable in quality from traditional public schools, with both having some strong results while sharing lingering problems related to social class and race.

Since charter schools have become the primary face for the accountability machine of education reform, embracing many of the primary policies and practices of the standards and high-stakes testing era, challenging charter schools must continue as a lever for overturning the entire accountability era.

The Beginning of the End?: Maintaining Hope

As the tide has turned against charter schools, many parents have also begun to reject high-stakes testing and embrace the opt-out movement, and the entire country has witnessed a jumbled but significant challenge to national standards, the Common Core.

In other words, many of the key aspects of major polices designed to reform public education have suffered eroding support from the public in general and parents specifically—even while the larger political environment has embraced an ugly form of right-wing ideology. Questioning charter schools must continue and must also fit into helping create a much different structure for education reform.

Therefore, recent challenges to charter schools and the reform agenda cannot be allowed to be swept away in the post-truth mayhem of Trumplandia.

Even Tough, who made much of his fame by supporting "no excuses" charter schools and "grit" has begun to backpedal, as seen in his latest book, *What Works and Why*, and recent public messages. And zero tolerance policies, so prevalent in charter schools, have been challenged by parents, the public, and even the Office of Civil Rights.

Once popular among educators and the media, both "grit" and growth mindset have lost favor as well, particularly as useful approaches to addressing vulnerable populations of students. As Paul Gorski, Associate Professor of Integrative Studies in New Century College at George Mason University and founder of EdChange, warns: "No set of curricular or pedagogical strategies can turn a classroom led by a teacher with a deficit view of families experiencing poverty into an equitable learning space for those families."[55]

And TFA, strongly linked with charter schools, has experienced multiple years of decline in applications, as well as cities and states dropping partnerships. Since TFA was touted as the quick and easy fix to a failed teacher workforce buoyed by teachers' unions, this decline signals yet more cracks in both education reforms promises as well as suggests a potential end to the era of accountability.

Challenges to charter schools by national organizations are simply catching up with, for example, Matthew Di Carlo's 2011 warning in "Explaining The Consistently Inconsistent Results of Charter Schools": "there is nothing about 'charterness' that leads to strong results."

Today, with powerful messages from the NAACP and BLM, activists supporting public schools must remain resolved to emphasize the overwhelming evidence that simply creating charter schools and implementing the same ineffective policies—new standards, new high-stakes tests, "grit," growth mindset, zero tolerance, TFA—has not and cannot create the sort of reform needed that addresses inequity of opportunities for the students who need public schools the most.

As well, activists supporting public schools must be vigilant about the utter failure of school choice, which is a form of zombie politics paralleling the accountability buffet of the past thirty years that has proven to be universally hollow as well.

The remaining hurdles, of course, include a well informed and vocal public as well as political leaders in office (consider Duncan's turn of attitude came after he left office) willing to question and then change their standard reform practices.

This now seems a Herculean task in post-truth Trumplandia— but hope has to overcome fatalism here. However, *the rise of Trumplandia was both gradual and sudden.*

In "The ambitious education plan of the Black Lives Matter movement," Emily Deruy writes in *The Atlantic* regarding Black Lives Matter's K-12 education agenda:

> "The education system in this country has never worked for poor people and people of color," said Rivera. "We're not calling for the status quo. We don't want things to continue as they've always done."

Ultimately, questions about charter schools and their advocates must continue and resonate in a way that recognizes an extremely complicated message about historical and current failures of public education—primarily the inequity of opportunity in the lives and schooling of black, brown, and poor students—that has not been and cannot be addressed by high-stakes accountability or through a form of schooling, charter schools, that simply houses failed policies.

Along with questioning charter support, Dixson and Perry call for reformers to change course in a way that serves communities—especially black and brown poor communities—instead of using those children and their education as political theater.

In post-truth Trumplandia, this imperative is even more urgent.

Charter schools like the entirety of the accountability era must be named for what they are: political theater.

Trumplandia as the ultimate and hollowest political theater cannot be allowed to win.

Along with U.S. politics, public education and education reform need a new script, and continuing resolved to stop charter schools and the accountability era can be an important moment in making that happen.

The Inevitable Rise of Trumplandia: Market Ideology Ate Our Democracy

Writing in 2000 specifically about education reform, Michael Engel[56] acknowledges: "Market ideology has triumphed over democratic values not because of its superiority as a theory of society but in part because in a capitalist system it has an inherent advantage" (p. 9).

Nearly four decades before Engel's claim, Raymond E. Callahan[57] confronted what he labeled the cult of efficiency in education:

> The tragedy itself was fourfold: that educational questions were subordinated to business considerations; that administrators were produced who were not, in any true sense, educators; that a scientific label was put on some very unscientific and dubious methods and practices; and that an anti-intellectual climate, already prevalent,

was strengthened. (p. 246)

What is disturbingly clear here is that despite the enduring claims that universal public education—often attributed to the idealistic foresight of Founding Father Thomas Jefferson—serves our democracy, public schooling has in fact worked almost entirely in the service of market ideology: sorting children for the workforce and instilling compliance in those young people become good and compliant workers, as Audrey Watters noted:[58]

> Although there is some lip service paid to learning computer programming in order to deepen students' thinking and expand their creativity, much of the conversation about computer science is framed in terms of developing students who are "job ready" – the rationale for teaching computer science President Obama gave in his final State of the Union address in January.

And here we have a subset of the entire country.

While many are wringing their hands about the post-truth U.S., our newly minted Trumplandia is not anything new, but the logical outcome of who we have always been—a belief culture skirting by on mythologies and false narratives to mask the ugly facts of our essential commitments to competition, consumerism, and capitalism.

Donald Trump is the best and most accurate personification of who the U.S. currently is, but also the embodiment of who we have always been.

Founded as a revolt against monarchy, the Founding Fathers used the rhetoric of freedom as a veneer for a few privileged men truly wanting the doors to exploitation, not closed, but opened just a tad wider so they could cozy in.

The newly founded free country allowed by law the enslave-ment of humans and the relegation of women to second-class citizenship.

"Life, liberty, and the pursuit of happiness" was post-truth.

Or at least only the sliver of truth for a select few white men already clutching power.

All you have to do is to listen *now or to the record of* black voices, women's voices, the voices of the imprisoned and impov-erished: "(America never was America to me.)"[59]

Just as the robber baron era of U.S. history[60] was no blip on the country's radar, but who we really are, the current ascension of Trumplandia is simply a more full unmasking of our complete failure at democracy and human liberation.

Trump's apparent cabinet appointments, his claims he doesn't need daily briefings, and the brash blurring of celebrity and huck-ster business acumen—these are the U.S. laid bare.

We have always been mostly branding—meritocracy, boot straps, upward mobility as marketing lingo with little basis in fact.

Political leaders have always sold the U.S. public a bill of goods wrapped in the American flag; George W. Bush sold a war on repackaged lies, and there were essentially only consequences for the soldiers, the U.S. public, and the victims of that war.

But the warmongers remain essentially unscathed.

And thus, Trump as Teflon blow-hard reality TV star/business huckster is just a few notches past Ronald Reagan as Teflon actor.

The ugliest paradox of all is that in our lust for consumerism we have allowed market ideology to eat our democracy, and as the metaphor requires, the excrement has really hit the fan this time.

Anything

I am exceedingly over-educated, well-read to an absurd extreme.

I am also too self-aware, introspective to the point of near paralysis.

And my fortune of privilege and leisure leaves me too much time to think about *everything*.

Broken, I lie here writing after having been handed an entirely new life not of my choosing, an accident in the first week of my holiday break probably redirecting a significant part of my life as a recreational cyclist.

That first week of recovery was consumed by pain and immobility, but I was not able to relax and read, although I thought that would be one positive to the situation.

This week, however, as most everyone has now returned to work, I find myself entirely alone. I resumed reading Chimamanda Ngozi Adichie's *Half a Yellow Sun*, a 2006 novel focusing on Nigeria during the 1960s.

Reading this essentially political novel in 2016-2017 has been chillingly prescient about the current U.S., and while I balk at the use of the term "universal" since it tends to be a veneer for normalizing privilege, Adichie's narrative often exposes the *enduring*.

In "Part Two: The Late Sixties", the section opens as the novel does with Ugwu, an Opi village boy who is a servant for a Nsukka University professor, Odenigbo. Several years have passed in the story, and Ugwu is temporarily back in his village:

> His visit home suddenly seemed much longer than a week, perhaps because of the endless grassy churning in his stomach from eating only fruits and nuts. His mother's food was unpalatable. The vegetables were overcooked, the cornmeal was too lumpy, the soup was too watery, and the yam slices coarse from being boiled without a dollop of butter. He could not wait to get back to Nsukka and finally eat a real meal. (p. 151)

This is a powerful scene in the context of the first paragraphs of the novel as Ugwu walks to Odenigbo's house to become his houseboy. Ugwu's aunt tells the boy, "'You will eat meat every day'":

> Ugwu did not believe that anybody, not even this master he was going to live with, ate meat *every day*. He did not disagree with his aunty, though, because he was too choked with expectation, too busy imagining his new life away from the village. (p. 3)

So as I was reading Adichie's dramatization of politics, privilege, and what *is* and *becomes* normal for anyone, I was reminded of Albert Camus's *The Stranger* and Meursault's thoughts from prison:

Afterwards my only thoughts were those of a prisoner....
At the time, I often thought that if I had had to live in
the trunk of a dead tree, with nothing to do but look
up at the sky flowering overhead, little by little I would
have gotten used to it. I would have waited for birds to
fly by or clouds to mingle, just as here I waited to see my
lawyer's ties, and just as, in another world, I used to wait
patiently until Saturday to hold Marie's body in my arms.
Now, as I think back on it, I wasn't in a hollow tree trunk.
There were others worse off than me. Anyway, it was one
of Maman's ideas, and she often repeated it, that after a
while you could get used to anything. (p. 77)

Much of my undergraduate time spent as a student-by-choice
focused on existential philosophy and literature, leading eventually to my discovering and embracing the educational writing of
Maxine Greene.

So as I recovered in the weeks leading to my 56th birthday—a
new year, a new age, and this new existence forced onto me—I was
deeply moved by "you could get used to anything."

Anything?

What an ugly thing to be human and having the capacity to
get used to *anything*.

But there was a time in the U.S. when slavery was perfectly
normal. There was a time in the world when the Holocaust was
perfectly normal.

Because *normal*, like *history*, is the province of those with
power, a way to render some Others "deliberately silenced,...pref-
erably unheard" (Arundhati Roy's "The 2004 Sydney Peace Prize

lecture").

And today the U.S. is eagerly normalizing a person and ideologies that would have seemed illegitimate just months ago.

As happened to Ugwu, will we in a few short years have our tastes so dramatically transformed that this bitter dish being served to us now will become what sates our hunger?

Franz Kafka's "A Hunger Artist" is a brief parable about the "art of fasting"—in which the artist becomes so transformed that he fasts himself to death, explaining:

> "Because I have to fast. I can't do anything else," said the hunger artist. "Just look at you," said the supervisor, "why can't you do anything else?" "Because," said the hunger artist, lifting his head a little and, with his lips pursed as if for a kiss, speaking right into the supervisor's ear so that he wouldn't miss anything, "because I couldn't find a food that tasted good to me. If had found that, believe me, I would not have made a spectacle of myself and would have eaten to my heart's content, like you and everyone else." Those were his last words, but in his failing eyes there was still the firm, if no longer proud, conviction that he was continuing to fast.

A gift of Kafka comes in the final paragraph when he offers the briefest of parables within a parable:

> "All right, tidy this up now," said the supervisor. And they buried the hunger artist along with the straw. But in his cage they put a young panther. Even for a person with the dullest mind it was clearly refreshing to see this wild animal prowling around in this cage, which had been

dreary for such a long time. It lacked nothing. Without having to think much about it, the guards brought the animal food whose taste it enjoyed. It never seemed once to miss its freedom. This noble body, equipped with everything necessary, almost to the point of bursting, even appeared to carry freedom around with it. That seemed to be located somewhere or other in its teeth, and its joy in living came with such strong passion from its throat that it was not easy for spectators to keep watching. But they controlled themselves, kept pressing around the cage, and had no desire at all to move on.

Like Ugwu, Meursault, the hunger artist—the panther "get[s] used to anything."

Kurt Vonnegut's Introduction to *Mother Night*, a work confronting a Nazi reality now again before humanity, begins: "This is the only story of mine whose moral I know. I don't think it's a marvelous moral; I simply happen to know what it is: We are what we pretend to be, so we must be careful about what we pretend to be" (p. v).

I am exceedingly over-educated, well-read to an absurd extreme.

I am also too self-aware, introspective to the point of near paralysis.

And my fortune of privilege and leisure leaves me too much time to think about *everything*.

I am afraid of who I have become, who I pretend to be, and if I too can "get used to anything."

And I am near to terrified of the same for the world around me.

You Don't Know Nothing: U.S. Has Always Shunned the Expert

Why did you listen to that man, that man's a balloon
"Friend of Mine," The National

My redneck past includes a childhood steeped, like the family formula for making sweet tea, in a demand that children respect authority—authority-for-authority's sake, the status of authority despite the credibility of the person in that status.

And is typical in the South, these lessons were punctuated with refrains such as the one my mother launched at us often: "He's a know-it-all that don't know nothing."

But the best laid plans of parents often go awry, and they certainly did for me because this aspect of my redneck past backfired big time, resulting in a life-long skepticism of authority as well as my own pursuit of expertise trumping status.

Among my most irritating qualities, I suspect, is I work very hard not to hold forth until I am well informed, but when I do hold forth, I am passionate and that passion often comes off as arrogance.

I have little patience with debating when the other side lacks credibility, and I also balk at the silliest of all—"We will agree to disagree, then."

Well, no, since your position has no credibility.

So I am particularly fascinated with what I consider a parallel interest currently with fake news and post-truth, what Tom Nichols calls "The Death of Expertise."

Nichols and his argument, coming from his conservative perspective, represent, I think, why expertise currently and historically has been marginalized in the U.S.

Pop culture, in fact, has documented well how the so-called average American finds expertise and being educated mockable— think Fonzie on *Happy Days* and Ross on *Friends*.

Uneducated Fonzie is always smarter than the educated, and Ross is a laughing stock among his friends, notably often one-upped by the very anti-intellectual Phoebe and Joey (I discuss the latter more fully in "Belief Culture").

Nichols and I share a concern about how little expertise matters in political and public discourse as well as policy, but while he and I share some elements of being experts, we are divided by our essential ideologies.

This presents a paradox: The U.S. rejects a cartoonish and monolithic "expert class," but most fields/disciplines have a fairly wide spectrum of stances within them (in other words, the "expert class" rejected by the U.S. simply doesn't exist).

But even that is oversimplified. Let me return to my redneck past.

In the South specifically, rejecting expertise is often about traditional views of respecting authority, best captured, I think, in how Huck Finn's father shames Huck for his book learning. Huck even confesses: "I didn't want to go to school much, before, but I reckoned I'd go now to spite papa" (*Adventures of Huckleberry Finn*, Mark Twain).

One of my former colleagues recounted often that his own father identified sending my friend to college was the worst mistake his father ever made.

Perversely, many see being informed, knowledgeable as rudeness, disrespectful.

A better recent confrontation of expertise than Nichols's, I think, is Freddie deBoer's "What Is Aleppo?," focusing on Gary Johnson:

> I would like to nominate Gary Johnson's infamous "What is Aleppo?" gaffe as the moment which, for me, most typifies 2016, at least as far as our intellectual culture goes.
>
> Predictably, and deservedly, Johnson was raked over the coals for this. A major presidential candidate — one who had far more electoral impact than Jill Stein, for instance — not knowing about this important foreign policy issue was disturbing. But it's essential to recognize what he actually got in trouble for. Johnson's great failure,

what actually fed his public humiliation, was not a lack of *knowledge*. It was a lack of *knowingness*.

deBoer argues: "Ours is a culture of cleverness, not of knowledge, one that is far more comfortable in assessing wit than in assessing evidence."

And here we may have a more accurate window into why someone who is not really an expert, such as Donald Trump, but is smug and cavalier about *being smart*, is more compelling in the U.S. than actual experts. Trump passes deBoer's test:

> That kind of thing: obviously smart but not, like, all try-hard about it. You are expected to work out relentlessly to train your body and to show everyone that effort, but your intelligence must be effortless, even accidental.

As I have argued, this is a very high-school popularity kind of dynamic in which bravado trumps credibility; again, think Fonzie's allure in pop culture: "See, the drop-out is smarter than all those teachers!"

My own career as an educator has highlighted these exact patterns.

As a teacher of English, I am not credible in the field of English because I am *just a teacher* with an undergraduate, Master's, and Doctorate in education (not English). However, to politicians and the public, I am routinely rejected in debates about education *because* my experience and expertise lie in education.

As a prelude to the rise of Trump, consider Arne Duncan, who has no degree in education and who has only experience in education as a political appointee.

Who do you think has more public and political influence on education—Duncan because of his statuses of authority or me with 33 years in education, an advanced degree, and a substantial publication history?

That question is nearly laughable in the U.S.

Let me end with a couple examples that are useful for a more nuanced consideration of the role of experts, grounded, I think, in deBoer's discussion.

First, consider Joseph R. Teller's "Are We Teaching Composition All Wrong?" and Doug Hesse's "We Know What Works in Teaching Composition," both published in *The Chronicle of Higher Education*.

I immediately blogged a rebuttal to Teller, "Is Joseph R. Teller Teaching Composition All Wrong?," and discovered through responses to my concerns that Teller has greater expertise in literature than composition (which I suspected).

Hesse's rebuttal is grounded in his *expertise in composition*, his status of authority (president of NCTE), and his appeal to disciplinary authority (citing ample research that accurately reflects the field of composition).

None the less, Teller's piece speaks to both an uniformed public and a click-bait culture, and it is likely, as John Warner mused on Twitter, that Hesse's *better piece* will not garner as many views or as much commentary as Teller's.

This debate between experts serves to highlight, again, the failure of media in terms of honoring expertise, but it also demonstrates that expertise is often narrow and that disciplines are more often contentious than monolithic (although there are some things that are essentially settled and no longer debatable).

Bluntly, we must admit that *simplistic* resonates more than *complex*—and expertise is not only narrow but also complex.

Finally, to highlight that expertise is as much about wrestling with knowledge as having knowledge, I offer a debate in a guest co-edited volume of *English Journal* (November 2016), centered on *The Adventures of Huckleberry Finn*:

- Editors' Introduction: Teaching *Adventures of Huckleberry Finn*: Essays in Conversation, Julie Gorlewski and David Gorlewski

- Huck and Kim: Would Teachers Feel the Same if the Language Were Misogynist?, Peter Smagorinsky

- The Irrationality of Antiracist Empathy, Leigh Patel

- Is *Huck Finn* Still Relevant? Revisiting "The Case for Conflict," Ebony Elizabeth Thomas

- We Dare Not Teach What We Know We Must: The Importance of Difficult Conversations, Jocelyn A. Chadwick

At one level, the experts included in this debate, in my informed opinion, are far more likely to have credible positions about the topic than people without degrees and experience in literature, the canon, race/racism, and teaching.

Yet, among these articles, you will find pointed disagreement—and as someone with expertise in these areas, I find myself siding with some, rejecting others, even as I respect the basic expertise among them all.

So today, we are faced with a historical and immediate problem, one that could be solved if we reconsidered our cultural antagonism toward expertise and embraced a greater appreciation for informed stances, the realm of the expert.

As a critical pedagogue, I appease my skepticism about authority and quest for expertise by honoring being authoritative over authoritarian (see Paulo Freire's *Pedagogy of the Oppressed*).

It is ours to resist extremes, neither ignoring experts nor abdicating all authority to experts.

As cumbersome as it may seem, democracy that honors all voices works well only when we start with the most informed voices and then allow "all voices" to occur in an educated space.

Currently, we are prisoners to bravado drowning out expertise, and in that echo chamber, freedom cannot survive.

References

1. White evangelicals voted overwhelmingly for Donald Trump, exit polls show, Sarah Pulliam Bailey 9 November 2016 *The Washington Post*

2. Matthew 19:24: "Again I tell you, it is easier for a camel to go through the eye of a needle than for someone who is rich to enter the kingdom of God."

3. CBS News Exit Polls: How Donald Trump won the U.S. presidency, Stanley Feldman and Melissa Herrmann 9 November 2016 *CBS News*

4. Why Trump Won: Working-Class Whites, Nate Cohn 10 November 2016 *The New York Times*

5. Why White High School Drop Outs Have More Wealth Than Black College Graduates, Matt Bruenig 24 October 2014 *Demos*

6. Equitable Growth Profile of the Research Triangle Region, Policy Link 2015

7. American women voted overwhelmingly for Clinton, except the white ones, Aamna Mohdin 9 November 2016 *Quartz*

8. 'This was a whitelash': Van Jones' take on the election results Josiah Ryan 9 November 2016 *CNN*

9. Newt Gingrich says poor kids have no work habits, suggest janitorial work (VIDEO), December 02, 2011, Freya Petersen

10. So, Newt's going to teach 'poor people' how to get a job? Democratic Underground.com

11. Prekindergarteners Left Behind: Expulsion Rates in State Prekindergarten Programs, Walter S. Gilliam, FCD Policy Brief Series No. 3 May 2005

12. "A league table of educational disadvantage in rich nations", Innocenti Report Card No.4, November 2002, UNICEF Innocenti Research Centre, Florence

13. "Child Poverty in Rich Countries, 2005", Innocenti Report Card No.6, UNICEF Innocenti Research Centre, Florence

14. "Child poverty in perspective: An overview of child well-being in rich countries", Innocenti Report Card No 7, 2007, UNICEF Innocenti Research Centre, Florence

15. The Racial Wealth Gap's Larger Than Ever. Here's How It Will Destroy Us, Kai Wright, *Truthout* 29 July 2011

16. Gingrich half-off on food stamps, Matt Smith, CNN

17. Measuring Donald Trump's supporters for intolerance, Lynn Vavreck

18. Hey white southerners, let's talk about our Confederate heritage, Matt Comer

19. Justice Scalia suggests blacks belong at "slower" colleges, Stephanie Mencimer, *Mother Jones*

20. Clarence Thomas Suggests Affirmative Action is Like Jim Crow, Elizabeth Flock, *US News & World Report*

21. A Captain America Comic Has Led to Online Chaos, Abraham Riesman, *Vulture*

22. *Teaching Comics Through Multiple Lenses*, Crag Hill, editor (Routledge)

23. McWilliams, O.C. (2009). Not just another racist honkey: A history of racial representation in Captain America and related publications. In R.G. Weiner (Ed.), *Captain America and the struggle of the superhero: Critical essays* (pp. 66-78). Jefferson, NC: McFarland and Company, Inc.

24. Brown, J.A. (1999, Spring). Comic book masculinity and the new black superhero. *African American Review, 33*(1), 25-42.

25. Hack, B.E. (2009). Weakness is a crime: Captain America and the Eugenic ideal in early twentieth-century America. In R.G. Weiner (Ed.), *Captain America and the struggle of the superhero: Critical essays* (pp. 79-89). Jefferson, NC: McFarland and Company, Inc.

26. Nama, A. (2011). *Super black: American pop culture and black superheroes*. Austin: University of Texas Press

27. Connors, S.P. (2013). "It's a bird … It's a plane … It's … a comic book in the classroom?": *Truth: Red, white, and black* as test case for teaching superhero comics. In P.L. Thomas (Ed.), *Science fiction and speculative fiction: Challenging genres* (pp. 165-184). Boston, Ma: Sense Publishers

28. Progressive Racism, feministkilljoys 30 May 2016 [blog]

29. There will never be another Muhammad Ali. Athletes today are too rich to take political risks, Karl Taro Greenfeld 10 June 2016 *Los Angeles Times*

30. The world saw a grieving mother. Donald Trump saw a Muslim, Amana Fontanella-Khan 1 August 2016 *The Guardian*

31. Ghazala Khan: Trump criticized my silence. He knows nothing about true sacrifice, 31 July 2016 *The Washington Post*

32. Trump: Tribune Of Poor White People, Rod Dreher 22 July 2016 *The American Conservative*

33. Republicans are confusing feelings with facts — and it's dangerous, Lisa Fogarty 24 July 2016 *She Knows*

34. Emdin, C. (2016) *For White Folks Who Teach in the Hood…and the Rest of Y'all Too: Reality Pedagogy and Urban Education*. Boston, MA: Beacon Press.

35. Paul Ryan responds to Donald Trump's misogyny, Matt Fuller 7 October 2016

36. 4 Ways To Challenge The Male Gaze, Kelsey Lueptow 27 May 2013 *Everyday Feminism*

37. 25 Everyday Examples of Rape Culture, Shannon Ridgway 10 March 2014 *Everyday Feminism*

38. #TBT: Reagan's 1980 convention speech calls to 'Make America Great Again' [VIDEO], Ryan Girdusky 14 July 2016 *Red Alert Politics*

39. Lost in Adaptation: Kurt Vonnegut's Radical Humor in Film and Print, P. L. Thomas, *Studies in American Humor*, New Series 3, No. 26, Special Issue: Kurt Vonnegut and Humor (2012), pp. 85-101

40. The Politics of Kurt Vonnegut's "Harrison Bergeron," Darryl Hatten-

hauer, *Studies in Short Fiction*, Vol. 35, No. 4 (Fall 1998)

41. Vonnegut and Labor, Matthew Gannon and Wilson Taylor 2 September 2013 *Jacobin*

42. Sex offender who chained up woman killed at least seven, say police, Associated Press 6 November 2016 *The Guardian*

43. 'This is horrifying': serial rape suspect's arrest rattles University of Wisconsin, Joanna Walters 30 October 2016 *The Guardian*

44. Why James Baldwin's The Fire Next Time Still Matters, Orlando Edmunds 2 November 2016 *JStor Daily*

45. 4 Ways To Challenge The Male Gaze, Kelsey Lueptow 27 May 2013 *Everyday Feminism*

46. Baldwin in the Obama Years, Scott Korb 4 November 2016 *Guernica*

47. The Myth of the Bad Teacher, Adam Bessie 15 October 2010 *Truthout*

48. Post-Election College Paper Grading Rubric, Daveena Dauber 11 November 2016 *McSweeney's*

49. Donald Trump's false comments connecting Mexican immigrants and crime, Michelle Ye He Lee 8 July 2015 *The Washington Post*

50. Research says there are ways to reduce racial bias. Calling people racist isn't one of them, German Lopez 15 November 2016 *Vox*

51. Whites See Racism as a Zero-Sum Game That They Are Now Losing, Michael I. Norton and Samuel R. Sommers, *Perspectives on Psychological Science* 6(3), 215–218

52. There is No "E" in Zombi Which Means There Can Be No You Or We, Roxane Gay 1 October 2010 *Guernica*

53. Exploring the consequences of charter school expansion in U.S. cities, Bruce D. Baker 30 November 2016 Economic Policy Institute

54. Excerpts From Bush's Speech on Improving Education 3 September 1999 *The New York Times*

55. Poverty and the ideological imperative: a call to unhook from deficit and grit ideology and to strive for structural ideology in teacher education, Paul C. Gorski, *Journal of Education for Teaching*, 42(4), 378-386

56. Engel, M. (2000). *The struggle for control of public education: Market*

ideology vs. democratic values. Philadelphia, PA: Temple University Press

57. Callahan, R. E. (1962). Education and the cult of efficiency: A study of the social forces that have shaped the administration of the public schools. Chicago: The University of Chicago Press

58. "Education Technology and the 'New Economy,'" Audrey Watters, December 2016, Hack Education

59. "Let America Be America Again," Langston Hughes

60. Zinn, H. (2015). *A People's History of the United States.* New York: Harper Perennial Modern Classics; Reissue edition (November 17, 2015)

Lightning Source UK Ltd.
Milton Keynes UK
UKOW01f1036220917
309680UK00009B/255/P